HomoSteading
at the 19th Parallel

HomoSteading at the 19th Parallel

One man's adventures building
his nightmare dream house on
the Big Island of Hawaii

David Gilmore

iUniverse, Inc.
New York Lincoln Shanghai

HomoSteading at the 19th Parallel
One man's adventures building his nightmare dream house on the Big Island of Hawaii

iUniverse books may be ordered through booksellers or by contacting:

iUniverse
2021 Pine Lake Road, Suite 100
Lincoln, NE 68512
www.iuniverse.com
1-800-Authors (1-800-288-4677)

ISBN: 978-0-595-45473-0 (pbk)
ISBN: 978-0-595-89785-8 (ebk)

Printed in the United States of America

For the restless wanderers forever searching for home

To commemorate my purchase of land in Hawaii
March 26, 2004

I want to go back the way I came
To drink water from the sky on my last day
To lie beside my beloved for a nap
And then to depart the world
in warm water
like I arrived
my transition, this time
witnessed only by the rain
washed away so gently from this life
and pushed from the surface of the earth
ever lightly by the generous hands of blue

—David Gilmore

CONTENTS

ACKNOWLEDGEMENTS

Like many Americans, I grew up in the suburbs with little connection to my neighbors other than a smile and wave coming and going. With their hedges and electric garage doors, the single-family ranch house is designed to keep people tucked away from and out of sight of each other. Even American building codes mandate such detached living, requiring houses to be set back far from the street, which often has no sidewalk. By design of such "communities," one is likely never to know one's neighbors. Ah, but that is America—a country so rudely diverse that we often don't really *want* to know our neighbors. What, after all, do I have in common with the people next door other than that our plat maps are rolled up next to each other at the county building office?

Building a house, however, in a remote, rural location on an island in the middle of the ocean requires a little extra community involvement. Your relations with your neighbors can make or break your construction project. What do you do when you need a bag of drywall nails and the nearest store is thirty-five miles roundtrip and gas is nearly $4 a gallon? What do you do when your phone is out, your Internet is down or there's questionable police and ambulance services? You go to your neighbors.

But sometimes, your neighbors come to you, as did the Building Angels, John Thomspson and Harlan Middleton. One steamy afternoon they walked by the construction site to introduce themselves and noticed I was struggling to clean up the myriad screw ups of the "drywall boys" (about whom you'll read later on). John and Harlan

are in their 50s and 60s respectively, and happened to be languishing in the quiet of their own post-construction doldrums.

Harlan came up to me and in his southern accent drawled,
"Here, hon, give me that trowel and let me show you how to do it."
He glopped some topping compound on a bare piece of drywall in a
closet and troweled it around. Dab, dab, dab. Trowel, trowel,
trowel. "Don't over work it or it's gonna look like hell. Now here,
you do, it and we'll continue our walk and come back and see how
you're doing." They continued on down the street dodging rain
showers.

They arrived back in twenty minutes by which time I had done
half a wall. Harlan admired my technique enthusiastically. After
many months of being severely criticized by every contractor who'd
tromped through these four bare walls, I was desperately hungry for
someone to just say, "Good job." I practically collapsed at his feet
with gratitude. *Finally* I had done something right!

John and Harlan both confessed they were a little bored and
added that if I needed any help with anything or needed to borrow
tools, I should feel free to call on them. That was their biggest mistake. I took them up on their offer of help. They came back, and
after texturing and drywalling with me for a couple hours each day
for about a week, they led me through bathroom wall building, glass
block installation, tiling, cabinet configurations and assembly, and
finally installing the upstairs flooring. They served it all up like a
couple of big southern waitresses working in a small town
diner—bitchy and campy all the way, but like true angels, they
never asked for a penny.

As a consequence of six weeks of helping me, they abandoned
their next building project. Harlan said to me over the phone one
day, "We have to thank you for reminding us how hard it is building a house, and you know, we're just of an age where we don't
want to take on another project like that." They cancelled their

appointment with the bulldozer. I felt a little guilty for having soured them on building their next house, but they insisted that it was all a blessing.

Another exemplary neighbor deserves special appreciation for his cheery assistance, his tireless encouragement, his knowledge of building, his trusty pickup truck and his DSL line. Oh, and the free watsu, massage, and naked dinner parties. Thank you, Bill Fultz, and sorry about your tile saw, but you wouldn't let me replace it. You were a font of building wisdom and a devoted friend despite your love of Barbra Streisand.

Thanks also to Don Falk for allowing me to stay in his jungalow at Kehena Beach while I got my house construction under way. (But, I must confess Don, I did use some bug spray one night. I hope you don't die of brain cancer.)

THANK YOU

Jean Sward, Gillian Kendall, Kimberly Dark, Rusty Kothavala, Scott Rebman, Scott Simmons, Richard Szubin, David Henry Sterry, Rob Zonfrelli, KiKi Dowdy, Ida Plotkin, Cathy Chestnut, Pat Maloy, Patrick Sweeney, Habib Krit, Flavia de Miranda, and Jeff Cotter for encouraging me to write; Jean Sward and Gillian Kendall for the fabulous editing and proofreading help; John Brennan for setting me up with a blog and a space for writing in Portland; Jean Sward for moral support and a gloriously nauseating helicopter ride; Patrick Sweeney for showing up, cooking great meals, and putting up with my tirades; Carl for blessing the land; Ernest and Jennifer Jackson for the food and cookies (sorry I wrecked your view); Kevin Horton for the building advice and tools; KiKi for a fabulous Thanksgiving dinner; Chewy for the post construction stress disorder (PCSD) therapy; Mark & Kathryn Phillips for your tools, building advice, and Christmas dinner; Craig

Lyman for doing my laundry and sneaking the game hens into the fridge; Richard Szubin for his worldly perspective; Sean Gilmore for reviewing my design plans; Craig & Tuko for being my last-minute best friends with lasagna; Lilia and Damian for their patience with the noise and dust; Chris Meintz for Monkey Pod's blanket and the loaner fridge; Richard Koob for providing space for events; Chris Williams for a shared love of pizza on rainy nights; Didier Flament for the wireless; Max for the gold leaf and the dinner parties; Rufus Wainwright for his comforting voice and his tormented heart—many a night I listened to him bleed so that I didn't have to; Richard Geddes for some neighborhood facts; Pat Maloy for forwarding my mail and watering the piano in Arizona; Kitty, Chris, and Rainer for keeping the house together in Hawaii; Mom & Dad for all the advice and the Sears gift certificate; Babs (wherever you are) for helping keep Bill in good humor; Kristal and Adrian for taking care of Monkey Pod (Yo, Adrian, thanks for letting me watch flies eat your staph infection); Henry for adopting my best friend; and Monkey Pod for the unconditional love and cuddles.

FOREWORD

By Kimberly Dark

David Gilmore's house blocks my view of the ocean.

I sat on my front lanai and watched his house being framed, walled, and finally its cute little roof perched atop it. Then I watched as he painted it a charming celery color with eggplant trim. Celery and eggplant? If I wanted to see those, I'd plant a garden. What I want to see is the sea.

Okay, the truth is, there's a lot of the sea to see from my front porch. My house is not quite a mile away from the watery blue world, so I still see glimpses of the reassuring blue around the houses and the trees. David's house is one of many that are now pocking the landscape, blocking my view!

Am I bitter? *Irritated?* Not really. This isn't Laguna Beach, California, after all, where the view is purchased along with the property and all of your neighbors have to agree if you plant a tree. This is the Puna District of Hawaii where your new neighbors might be chickens and goats—or people with chickens and goats. Or people who make noises like chickens and goats! Weirdo, eccentric white people (and a few other races), as far as the eye can see: that's our little rural subdivision. David fits right in (though he'll try to claim he doesn't), and so do I.

I have never in my life felt more at home than I do on Hawaii, in lower Puna. The book you are holding does not describe *the* Lower Puna. But it describes *one* Lower Puna: David's. And because he's a wonderful writer, you'll enjoy his Puna. No. Because he's a wonderful writer and *also* a gay, intellectual curmudgeon with a wry sense of humor and an array of experiences that range from bawdy to contemplative. You'll be happy with his Hawaii—but not always comfortable. Comfortable, but not always happy. This is David's perch upon the unpredictable paradise of Puna.

While I'm not bitter that he put up yet another house in between my lanai and the ocean, I *am* worried. I'm worried that excessive home building is hurting our little piece of paradise and that the delivery of American culture to this gentle Polynesian land is deeply wrong. Oh sure, America has "owned" Hawaii for quite some time now—but not Lower Puna.

The subdivision where David and I are neighbors got electricity less than ten years ago. Traditionally, this has been jungle, rainforest, and farmland. While David has not interviewed them for his book, I will tell you that spirits dwell here, and we're pushing them out—David and I, and our sort. We're pushing the spirit of the jungle out of Lower Puna while we push out the Hawaiian culture as well. I don't think the Hawaiians would've done that, but then, who's to know. Civilization has no rewind button.

And this is not a story about the jungle or the sea or the nature spirits. That would be *my* story of Lower Puna. David's is the story of the seeker—the home-seeker, the love-seeker, and the self-seeker. And I love him for writing this story because perhaps it means you won't have to come here and build your house in between the sea and me! You'll love this book, I promise. And it probably won't be only because the stories are funny and clever and give you a glimpse of a life you may not have. David's writing will touch you: You with the lust for travel and conquest; You the insecure and searching; You the paradise hunter. Let it happen. Enjoy yourself.

PRELUDE TO A DREAM

There is one thing you must know about me: there's a very good chance that at any given moment, I am going to bolt—that I will leave without any formal closure, and once I have left, you may never see me again. Knowing how to quickly locate and use the escape hatch has been the principal skill in my survival kit since the beginning.

You see, I was a delicate gay boy growing up in semi-rural, semi-civilized, inland Florida—the part of the peninsula that no one really cares to know about from one's sandy beach vacation or family trip to Disneyworld. One particular little town called Fort Myers, the east end of which was sandwiched between I-75 and nothing, served as the backdrop of my early life. Unlike coastal Florida, East Fort Myers with its constricting gene pools, used car dealerships, and abandoned department stores was mostly home to Florida natives. "Crackers" they called themselves—folks who shot and ate squirrels, mothballed cars in their front yards, and had a tire or two placed on each roof. (Were they to keep the roof from rattling in the wind or some sort of white trash Passover ritual—a tire on each roof and the angel of good taste would pass right on over?) East Fort Myers is the town that tourists forgot—something so enviable for one who has tried his whole life to do just that.

As a young man, I floated through that decidedly unglamorous landscape in a protective bubble of my own construction—a near-perfect world of romance, fine wine, night-blooming jasmine, smiling cowboys with starched white shirts, all set to a schmaltzy musical score of Chopin's nocturnes, played by me, the skinny kid at the piano. But every now and then, when my bubble drifted too far from home and was breached by the guns and tobacco chewing reality of my acrid childhood, it was essential to find the exit and find it fast. If you didn't have an exit, you dreamed one up. As soon as I was old enough to take care of myself, I bolted.

Subsequently, I have become a restless adult with an admittedly fractured sense of home. My life, although no longer replete with rednecks, seems perpetually dull and in need of a little zshushing. I left Florida at twenty-one on a quest for a new home in New York. At twenty-three, I drove west to San Francisco once again seeking a deeper sense of home that I didn't find in New York. A decade later and I'm once again fleeing—this time to Tucson from the foggy climes of Northern California in 2001. Alas, after four years of desert living, Arizona was starting to seem like a broken place—a barren land where people rubbed their dreams out in the sand. My discontent had reached an intolerable level and thus I resurrected an old skill—a familiar one: I would build my escape pod, climb aboard, and promptly float away from my less than fabulous, post-peak, midlife mediocrity like Glinda the Good Witch.

Lather, rinse, repeat.

Fast forward to a year after the final inspection of the Hawaii house. I now sit in my house in Arizona, unable to summon the interest to ever return to Hawaii. So, what went wrong? Instead, it would be easier to tell you what went right. What went right was the barn-raising community effort to put up the house—the little miracles that were worked by the various neighbors who tucked me under their wings, making food for me, offering a comforting word of encouragement or advice. Neighbors who had previously built gave me leftover nails or sold me their glass block at half-price—like a baby shower and I was receiving the construction hand-medowns. And of course, meeting my four-legged friend on the road one night—Monkey Pod as he came to be known—a lost black Lab I adopted. His appearance seemed like divine intervention at a very difficult time.

Still, I have not answered my own question: What went wrong? Well, that is the subject of this book. You'll read for yourself that perhaps the biggest failures were my own sensitivity and naïveté. I arrived in Hawaii an idealist—a stranger in a strange land, ready to take on my new role as *owner-builder*—an unglamorous title for what I thought would be a more lustrous adventure. I clearly had no idea what I was getting into. Hawaii is not a place that opens her arms and welcomes just anyone. Nor is the building industry particularly warm and fuzzy to the novice. Both expect you to pay your dues. Until such time that you're broken and desperate, prostrating yourself before Pele and the construction trades that have complete control of your life, you'll get no sympathy.

When you're a vacationer, your friends or your tour guide will meet you at the breezy airports of Hawaii, throw a string of fragrant tuberoses around your neck and welcome you with a smiling "aloha." But beneath that Hawaiian greeting comes an unspoken expectation and hope among many locals that when you are done with your vacation, you will leave. Who can blame them? Europeans arrived over two hundred years ago bearing smallpox that killed thousands of Hawaiians, mosquitoes and livestock that ate nearly all the native flora, and mongooses that finished off the native bird populations. It's an understatement to say that the day Captain James Cook sailed into Kealakekua Bay was not a good one for Hawaii. Now Hawaii is an occupied nation, taken over by the United States to protect its pineapple and sugar cane interests and with the foresight of a military base in the mid-Pacific region. Now it is America's 50th state.

And to this day, there is a palpable resentment toward the haoles—the foreigners, "those who do not breathe," the dead, the white people … me. Ironically, I found the strongest resentment of the haoles from other haoles who, perhaps in their own attempt to assuage their guilt for their own footprint on the land, turned their anger on the newly-arriving white folks. That is, after all, what America does best—claim a thing or a place and then unpack a ferocious sense of entitlement upon the next person wanting the same things. The scars on Hawaii cut deep and those of us just arriving face the ire of a disenfranchised local population.

At times my construction site became a boxing ring of haole versus local, building veteran versus rookie—a proving ground that bored holes in my psyche like the Roto Hammer that I learned to use. Ah, but all this would not have been enough to send me packing. I could have recovered, walled myself off after the last surly building inspector came to scrutinize my work with a measuring tape and level. I could have fortified my liquor cabinet, engaged the services of a good therapist and shed the nightmares of building one by one—from putting on the roof in a tropical storm, to watching GemSeal suck the nap off my rollers and forever embed them in my concrete floor. I could have let it all go.

So then, what was it that had me run screaming back to the mainland? Why didn't I stay to enjoy the beautiful tropical home that I so painstakingly built? Truth be told, I was as lonely as a male coqui frog in a treetop singing for a mate. A disproportionately high percentage of loony-tunes camped out in the neighboring jungles, stoned out of their minds playing the theme song to *The Flintstones* on the saxophone, and the narcissistic recreation of mainland gay culture left me feeling that I was stuck in the middle of the ocean with only my dog for company, pathetically unable to afford the high price of olives and goat cheese. Hell, I tell you. Pure homo hell.

A Few Notes to the Reader …

This book is based on the journal entries I posted to my blog www.nineteenthparallel.com and sent to a list of friends and family as time permitted me to write on rainy nights between bouts of construction. You'll notice that I signed each journal entry "Seaweed" or "Tumbleweed." I adopt geographically specific nicknames that I loosely use to describe myself in the new locale.

You'll notice that as the construction intensified with my builder disappearing forever (with my blueprints on his dashboard), the period between journal entries became longer. My line of credit began to run out, and with no builder to be found, every detail of the second half of the construction fell into my own hands. I spent more time hauling lumber and less time writing, and then when I did write, my blog became the repository of a huge amount of raw emotion.

You'll see how my enchantment with Hawaii turns to bitterness. In the face of hardship, I lost my naïve idealism and sense of adventure. I longed for a push-button life with regular trash pickup and all those suburban trappings from which I had previously bolted. I was clearly showing signs of PCSD—post construction stress disorder.

As a result, I lost ten pounds (weighing in at 125 pounds at the end) from long hours without food and hard labor carrying bags of concrete and innumerable buckets of topping compound up a flight of stairs. My body turned into a lean construction machine while my mind turned Captain Ahab, hell-bent on that final building inspection. I dropped boards on my toes and even sawed through two fingers one crazed afternoon trying to finish the trim by myself. Limping and spewing blood, I remained fixated on my own version of the Great White Whale. I gritted my teeth and finished working with the remaining fingers. Friends were becoming concerned that the house was going to destroy me. I was more concerned that my stores of Xanax were running out.

Finally, the day came and the building truly was over. I hauled the last pile of debris to the dump and put the last coat of paint on the lanai ceiling. But it was over for me like Vietnam was over for a veteran. Truly, the hardest part was just beginning: the silence of an empty house.

In the quiet after the maelstrom, I spent many nights swinging in my hammock with Monkey Pod nuzzled on my chest, taking stock of my life as a forty-something single gay man in a community where there was little hope of finding romantic companionship. The house failed to attract the man I hoped it would. Every man I met seemed to be there for just a brief spell, part of a naked yoga retreat or some wide-eyed gay adventure travel, and then voila!—I was back in the hammock with Monkey Pod, watching the twinkling lights of the cruise ships gliding silently by in the darkness.

I also came to realize that at my age, I looked better in a black turtleneck seated at a grand piano than sitting naked on a beach hiding my copy of the *Harvard Gay and Lesbian Review,* trying to find the rhythm in a group of stoned hippies in a drumming circle. My idealistic views of Hawaii as paradise were swept away from me like a rogue wave taking away my beach blanket and my clothes, leaving me stranded, naked, and in shock.

This book is more than a tome of the construction of a house. Building, in and of itself, is nothing that unusual or interesting, really. This book is, rather, an irreverent, often cynical account of Hawaii, her quaking land, and the quirky people that inhabit her as seen from the eyes of a newcomer. My year in Hawaii delivered all the adventure I signed on for, but it damn near ruined me.

Of course I did learn a few things, and if *that* is the measure of success, then, yes the project was successful. I eventually regained the use of all my fingers and put those ten pounds back on. I even learned a few things: lefty-loosey and righty-tighty work for everything except propane tanks, and "pigtails" are not just for hair.

There is light now in the middle of that once dark lava field at the 19th parallel. A passing daydream became a plan and raw materials became a house which today stands strong and protective in howling windstorms and earthquakes without even so much as a creak. A vegetable garden feeds its inhabitants. Phones and Internet connected that spot of once barren land to the world and the house became a stage for human life—someone else's.

Still, I hope you enjoy the adventure.

(Oh. Some of the names have been changed to protect the guilty.)

1

February 2004

A POSTAGE STAMP OF PARADISE

Before beginning a hunt, it is wise to ask someone
what you are looking for before you begin looking for it.
—*Pooh's Little Instruction Book,* inspired by A. A. Milne

In 1997 in the dead of winter, I visited a strange and wild place: the Puna District of the Big Island of Hawaii. The Big Island, if you've never visited, is the youngest and largest of the Hawaiian Archipelago, at the end of 1600 miles of islands in the middle of the Pacific Ocean making it technically the most remote island chain on earth. It boasts the southernmost point of the United States, if you consider Hawaii the United States. The air is the cleanest in the world. Much of the land is bare, black lava jutting out into the water, the landscape cast in hues of preternatural green, sapphire blue, and jet black.

My friend Jean and I ventured to the wet side of the island on vacation from San Francisco. Driving over from the dry side of the island, which was clogged with traffic and stripped of any signs of old Hawaii, we were delighted to find Puna so unpopulated and lush. There seemed to be some respect for Hawaiian traditions, as it had not yet been overrun with tourists.

Endless rainstorms quickly doused our glee. It wasn't raining cats and dogs. It wasn't raining buckets or any other metaphor for a deluge. It was raining waterfalls that seemed to follow us around wherever we went. We couldn't sleep with the lightning and thunder and the pounding rain on the metal roof of our rental cottage. Our clothes soon began to smell of mildew and roaches scurried about our room at night looking for food. After a week of this Hawaiian water torture, Jean and I ran screaming back to the mainland and I swore I would never, *ever* return to Puna, that is until I met Don Falk in San Francisco in the summer of 2003.

Don was the boyfriend of a friend—a distant connection but a guy who is immediately likable. He had just vacationed in Puna where he bought a funky beach house for a shockingly small sum of money. He excitedly showed us the pictures on his laptop. Over time, Don and I became friends and I grew more fascinated by his purchase. I would call him and listen to stories of his new life in the jungle. Always keeping exit strategies in mind, I tucked away the information for future use.

Don and his then boyfriend Max invited me to come and visit in Hawaii. My interest was piqued by the invitation and I asked them if they would host my 40th birthday party. I invited my ex-boyfriend Patrick to join me and we made the trip over in February 2004. Little did I know that on the last day of this decidedly less rainy vacation at Don's funky little jungalow, that Patrick and I would be buying a piece of property there as well.

After two weeks of birthday celebrations, snorkeling, watercoloring by the roiling sea, hiking the lava flows, and watching the evening rains shower the palm trees, we were seduced. This time around the weather has been considerably milder than my trip in

1997. Everyone said the rain we experienced then was due to a tropical storm (not their typical weather) and so my harsh opinion of Puna softened. Still I was not thinking of buying land in Hawaii in any serious way.

Near the end of our trip, Don mentioned that we could buy a lot in the Seaview neighborhood for around $10,000. We were driving along the coast when he sprung this thought on us—I was in the front seat, Patrick in the back. I remember the moment looking at Patrick in the rearview mirror of the car—as we were driving past the neighborhood when my eyes popped open.

"Really, $10,000!? How can that be? Patrick, what do you think? Want to go home with a little piece of the rock?" I watched his furrowed brow as we drove past Seaview. His look out the window at the idyllic grassy green park with swaying palms was asking, "Do I want to own *this?*"

He looked back at me and said, "Well if it's only $10,000, I'd consider it for an investment." Patrick never jumps on board with an emphatic YES! He will scratch his head and consider all possible outcomes before leaping to do anything. I usually operate quite the opposite.

With no time to waste before we were back on the plane to the mainland, Patrick and I obtained a self-guided realtor's map with a list of available properties. We were stunned to see a list of about fifty properties, half of which were priced under $25,000, many of which were indeed priced around $10,000, depending on proximity and view of the ocean. Bulldozed into a gentle sloping amphitheater with the ocean at center stage, Seaview has many lots within sight of the sea, hence the neighborhood's name.

Lava-damaged land goes cheap in Hawaii. Lots in Seaview consist of 7,500 square feet of land: 60 by 125 foot pieces of crumbly basalt formed in 1955 when the volcano Kilauea opened up a vent just uphill from the site. When the lava begins to flow, it destroys everything in its path: roads, water, sewer, power, and phone lines. It can turn a town into a smattering of houses cut off from everything and every one. Naturally, people are a little skittish about owning property in recently active lava flow. Seaview was recovering from its mid-century lava flow and had been incorporated as a subdivision in 1971 by the General Hawaiian Development Corporation. Over the years, real estate speculation toyed with Seaview's property values creating land grabs and land dumps tied to the vicissitudes of the global financial markets.

In Don's rusty 1990 Toyota Corolla we nicknamed "Boner," we drove around the barren streets cut into the lava field looking for a suitable lot. We passed unbelievably thick jungle lots teeming with mosquitoes, derelict lots with junked cars, broken-down, moss-covered school buses inhabited by scary white folk. Jacked-up cars and boats blocked the side streets. It was American suburbia shot through with post-apocalyptic, *Mad Max* aesthetics. I half expected Tina Turner and Mel Gibson to come swinging out of the jungles on vines to chase us away with machine guns.

We quickened our pace back out to the barren fields of lava where no trees had survived the lava flow. All seemed peaceful and calm out in the open. We stopped by one lot listed for $10,000. There were a few decent houses to the west of it—which meant potentially reasonable neighbors—something I was beginning to notice was a premium in Seaview. The rest was all undeveloped. There was nothing at all across the street—that would mean an ocean view until someone else built in front. The lava was covered with shin-high ferns and wild orchids blooming with small, magenta and white fragrant flowers.

We got out and kicked around a bit in the howling trade winds. The unevenness of the lava could twist your ankles if you weren't careful. We admired the blue ocean with white caps downhill about a mile. I couldn't quite hear the ocean, just the sound of wind in the ferns.

Breaking the silence of my own daydreaming I asked Patrick, "What do you think, Sweets? Jungle or lava?" He was busy crunching around the lava examining the orchids. He scratched his head nervously and chose his words carefully.

"I think that we don't have to find the perfect lot because it's just an investment, and it will be easier to sell a lot that doesn't need clearing for construction and that has an ocean view."

My crumple button had just been pressed, but I didn't let on. He was thinking investment, and I was already pretty well along in my Hawaiian dream house fantasy. I could see a three-story Polynesian bungalow with widow's walk, my wetsuit hanging on the lanai after a day of swimming with dolphins, making love in a hammock with my new Hawaiian boyfriend while the tropical breezes tickled our chest hairs and we enjoyed fresh, grilled ahi with mango roulade afterward.

It's a bit impractical to build a water-catchment roof with a widow's walk unless you intend to be airlifted onto it each afternoon; making love in a hammock is damn near impossible without getting elbowed in the face; and Hawaiian guys don't have chest hair. The ahi with mango roulade was probably the one salvageable detail of my fantasy. I snapped out of it to meet Patrick on firmer ground.

With surprisingly little discussion, Patrick and I came to an agreement and decided on the lot. Hawaiians have strong beliefs in the ancient lore of Pele, the goddess of fire who lives in Kilauea, the nearby volcano whose eruptions had sent smothering lava over this land some fifty years ago. We looked up the street name in a friend's Hawaiian dictionary and found out it meant "mysterious cold wind from Kilauea." I wondered if this was an omen of my involvement in this land: a cold wind would blow down from the volcano one day—perhaps the cold shoulder of Pele. Hmmm. At least it didn't mean hot lava flowing over the haole's house.

Patrick and I called the realtor and asked him to come down from Pahoa, the nearest town. The lot next door had sold in 1979 for $9,800, more than we were offering twenty-five years later. So we knew it was somewhat of a risky investment.

We put an offer of $9,500 on the lot and signed the papers on the tailgate of Richard Geddes' car. We waited breathlessly to find out if our offer was accepted. Later that afternoon, the phone rang at Don's house where we were staying. Don called out to me in the garden that the phone was for me from Pahoa Realty.

"They've accepted your offer," Richard told me with a little chuckle. Wow. It was that easy. No loan, no credit checks. We simply wrote personal checks and FedExed them later from the mainland, and in six weeks we were officially Hawaiian, at least in deed. Of course, as everyone finds out, there is more to being Hawaiian than being the deed holder of a piece of land.

I had a few moments of pause thinking about the entitlement that Americans have to this land that was technically an occupied nation—but then again—wasn't all of America? What could I possibly do about that now? The land does not know it has changed hands, so I figured I would deal with the scars of imperialism another time and at a slower pace. The fervor of having found a genuine bargain or that clichéd "slice of paradise" (or so we thought) was intoxicating. We both left my Hawaiian birthday celebration feeling like a new chapter had been opened. Before leaving, I dropped off sprouting coconuts at the perimeter of the lot and hoped to come back some day to find towering trees bearing fruit.

Taking off from the Hilo airport and out over the big blue at dawn, my mind ticked off the ideas of what to do with this land. Patrick returned to San Francisco, and I returned to Tucson, and then we both sort of forgot about it. The question of the property became relegated to a small back corner of my mind—something to think and dream about in quiet moments. A year and a half later, knowing little more than lefty-loosey, righty-tighty, I would be returning to this airport to build a house of my own design in this far-away corner of Hawaii.

2

Winter 2004 to Spring 2005

CIRCLES IN THE SAND

The world is round and the place which may seem like the end
may also be only the beginning.
—Ivy Baker Priest

The return home to Tucson was a bit of a letdown, as one would expect coming home from an extended 40th birthday celebration in Hawaii. But more than that, I was coming home becalmed—as if I had come down from a psychedelic trip to resume my life grudgingly as a mortal. I had recently retired from producing and hosting my national radio show, *Outright Radio*—a creative project that gave me a sense of purpose and creative focus. After seven years, exhausted by the fundraising imperative of a non-profit, I retired the show.

Rather than grieve the end of the radio show fully, in the summer of 2004, I turned my attention to filmmaking—what I thought was a natural progression from radio. (At the time, I didn't realize how much more lucrative public radio was compared to independent filmmaking.) The net result of my six-month, do-it-yourself crash course in low-budget filmmaking was a twenty-minute documentary called *Ideal Man*—a personal look at gay male body image obsessions. Jesse Rose DeRooy, the editor of the radio show, and I produced it together in her studio in Santa Cruz. The film delayed for us both the sense of loss from the demise of the radio show. The film made its way around the gay film festival circuit and on line.

Once the filming and editing in California was complete, I headed back to Tucson and this time was really confronted with the absence of any creative focus. Over the years, various projects and conjugal trips to California kept me from the nagging reality that I was basically a coastal California guy living in a desert of strip malls and white trash—a reality one never has to face in coastal California. Never one to blend in with my environment, I fancied myself an ex-pat Californian, some sort of artist-in-exile, and always made sure I had an airline ticket in the drawer.

To quell my boredom, late at night I would go on line and look at Hawaiian real estate. I was shocked and delighted to see that over the months since Patrick and I had stumbled upon our 7,500 square feet of jagged lava, our little property had doubled, tripled, quadrupled, and quintupled in value. We had entered the fray in February 2004, fortuitously just prior to another big land grab.

Alas, with the run on property, it also became clear that if I were ever to live in Hawaii—a thought that kept entering my mind with increasing frequency—I would be forced to build a house. The island housing market had priced me out entirely. Shacks that were once giveaways were now getting upwards of $200,000. Decent but modest homes were now fetching $300,000. It was beginning to look like the San Francisco Bay Area all over again, except this time I had my foot in the door.

Never one to stew in my discontent for years, I hatched my Tucson escape plan: get a home equity loan on the Tucson house (interest rates were about 6%) and build a house on the land we'd just bought in Hawaii. I would indulge my restlessness nature and start over in Hawaii. For the purposes of self-restraint, I promised I would go to Hawaii and spend at least a month there first, just to check it out and audition it as a place to live. I thought I would live in Hawaii if not full time, at least when Tucson was uninhabitable which, quite frankly, is most of the year. While people's high heels were melting into the pavement in the Arizona summer, I would be swimming with dolphins off the southern coast of Hawaii.

Self-restraint was at this point lip service. I had already made up my mind. I could no longer stand the mediocrity of Tucson. I couldn't bear trying to tune out the blight of urban sprawl, and I had failed to assemble a coven of art fags with which to conspire. Nice people seemed more interested in alcohol-free potlucks and pinochle night at the gay café than in the more irreverent charades on which I thrive. I booked my flight to Hawaii for the audition.

Returning to Hawaii in February 2005, I spent the month surveying the property, walking it, standing at the four corners, photographing it, measuring it, pacing back and forth on the lava. There was really nothing loveable about the land. The ground was sharp—it would slice your fingers open if you touched it. It was harsh and strangely barren in a place with so much rain and jungle. With nearly six feet (yes, *feet*) of rain annually, you would think there would be a teeming jungle there. But the lava holds no water and dirt is a precious commodity in Hawaii, making it the cleanest place on earth. Without dirt, there is no mud—just crumbled cinder. Everywhere. I was disappointed to see that the coconut palms I placed at the back corners of the lot a year prior had barely grown a foot—stunted by the lack of good soil.

Toward the front of the property there was one tree—a scruffy old ohia tree with a few red blossoms—a Hawaiian native plant that is usually the first to colonize a fresh lava flow. I vowed that if I built, I would work around the one tree. It stands alone today in front of the house as a kind of unflinching greeter to the property.

I began working through design concepts in my head while sitting on the beach, then on the backs of moldy envelopes, then in my graphics programs on my laptop. Each afternoon I would drive to the Kalani Internet café and send Patrick an email with my thoughts. I walked around the neighborhood, stopping at houses to interview anyone who seemed friendly to a passerby. Most of the people I talked to had more money than I and had so complicated their lives with construction details that they had lost their sense of joy. Living in "paradise"—a mainlander concept—didn't seem to be wearing terribly well on them. I heard of couples splitting up over the construction or when the house passed final building inspection. The owners were too mentally and physically exhausted to enjoy the house, and as a result sold it and left the island forever. I was convinced that this would *never* happen to me if I kept it simple.

I stood at the edge of the property one afternoon and made a short video clip for Patrick that said, "You know Patrick, it's a small lot and whatever we do, we have to do it simple and small ..." I should have returned to that video. I too fell into the trap believing that cheap interest rates meant a more fabulous house. And that the more fabulous the house, the bigger piece of paradise I would chisel off for myself.

3

Spring 2005

FLY AWAY

The journey of a thousand miles
begins with one big, fat home equity loan.

Where does one begin the task of floating away in an escape bubble?
One must first design the bubble. Thus I began, toward the end of
my exploratory month in Hawaii, to craft the first plan for the
house. It was to be two pods: a front pod and a back pod, linked
together with a roof and a common outdoor bathhouse. I drew it all
up to scale in Quark Xpress—a graphics program normally used for
designing books.

I could see now that what started out as a very simple idea—perhaps a modern-day version of the little grass shack in
Kealakekua—was taking a turn toward the grandiose. I met with
Tod Pritchett, a draftsman in Hawaiian Paradise Park. He drove
with me to the site and we looked at roofs along the way, stopping
in at one house that my design was loosely modeled after. Tod
seemed very professional and knowledgeable and signed on for the
job, though I had some reservations about him when I saw a signed
picture of George W. Bush above his office desk. I put aside my val-

ues for the sake of a good tradesman. He would draw up the plans from my sketches and I would review them by email from the mainland.

Before I left Hawaii that February, I arranged for the surveying pins to be located and the lot to be bulldozed flat. I stood by with my camera and tape measure as Justin, the gorgeous Japanese-Italian pin finder, scratched around the corners of the lot with a small rake in the places where pins should be. He managed to uncover one at the front left corner of the lot. Then, shooting a transit diagonally across, he pinpointed the spot where his assistant should dig for the next one. He located the right rear one, rusted and buried under about six inches of crumbling lava. Once you have found two, the rest are easy to find.

Later on, my new friend Carl came by to do a blessing of the land. We stood in the middle of the lot with collected ti leaves, (a Hawaiian tradition), while he sang some chants in Hawaiian. Where had this haole homo learned these? I suppose he could have been stringing together a bunch of vowels with H's and K's and I would have believed he was chanting in Hawaiian, but knowing Carl's integrity, it had to be legitimate. We braided the ti leaves and placed one bundle at each corner of the lot.

To finalize the ritual, I hiked out with my friend Max to see the lava flowing into the ocean just west of Kaimu. I brought along some red seedpods from palm trees to offer as a sacrifice to Pele. I tossed them into the glowing hot lava, expecting them to burst into flames, and silently I asked Pele for permission to build the house. Oddly, they did not ignite. They just sat there. How strange, I thought. Doesn't everything go up instantly in smoke? I took this as a very positive sign that she would not burn my house down if I built. I figured it was worth the asking and I was pleased with the answer.

Finally, on the last day of my trip, the old bulldozer arrived on a flatbed truck with its sandy-blond porn-star looking driver, Lance. The dozer was a vintage D7 that appeared to have been a World War II leftover. I stood on the street directing as Lance graded the property down to a buildable lot, creating an island mound in the front that would be a flowerbed encircled by a driveway. Afterward, I handed the lithe young driver a small fistful of cash and watched him load up the D7 onto the truck and drive away. We had broken ground, polluted the air and destroyed the ferns and orchids—a sight I've seen repeated many times in Hawaii. Not a single tree was taken down though, which was not a terribly laudable feat considering there was only one tree to start with.

I returned to Tucson and began the electronic correspondence with Tod the draftsman. Patrick was in Tucson finishing up renovations on an investment house with me. He stood by in my office watching as I designed and would, on occasion, interject a thought. I sent the PDF off to my architect brother Sean in Florida who gave me his thoughts: put in solid-core doors (louvered in the closets for airflow); specify awning windows that could remain open in the rain; and design a glass wall that would open up on the leeward side upstairs. Sean's suggestions were all excellent ones for a tropical house in the trade winds where you want to maximize airflow for mildew management—even if it's raining.

Don chimed in with a suggested re-design of the roofline. Originally I had sketched a shed roof, but with Don's urging, I switched to a more elegant Balinese-style roof that looked like either a big sunhat or a manta ray. This design made all the difference in the house's smile value and curb appeal.

The first draft he sent included the square footage, which was now up to 2,200! His bill for the drawings, based on the footage, was beyond my range of affordability. And so I opened his files in

Photoshop and began hacking away and humbling the project. I cut the back pod, the covered walkway, and the common bathhouse. The pared-down house now was 1,100 square feet with 500 square feet of lanai space—a two-story bungalow with slab floor. The bathroom and bedroom were to be downstairs with the kitchen and office upstairs, the laundry room outside, and an open-air staircase on the leeward side where the constant trade winds and rain would be blocked by the house.

As my thinking progressed, it dawned on me that I could put a bathroom on each floor and then rent one out if I needed the cash. So in another email, I instructed Tod to add a bar area to the downstairs that could be used as a makeshift kitchen and a bathroom upstairs, making each floor a complete unit.

Patrick continued his characteristic lip-biting and head-scratching, peeking in my office door as I went into late hours on my computer working it all out, taking files Tod would send, opening them in Illustrator, then Photoshop, marking them up and returning them as PDF files. It was remarkable to be able to design a house by email. Patrick made one small adjustment to the exterior, adding wings to the ground floor lanai to break up the imposing vertical lines as seen from the side. It was a good suggestion.

Tod incorporated Sean's ideas and sent me back a final draft of the house. It was looking adorable with attractive lines and proportions—an aerie of sorts. It looked like a house that would make you want to drive by just to take a look.

I sent Tod a check for his drafting work. He made his drawings into blueprints and had them reviewed and stamped by Hawaii architect Robert Smelker, and then he walked the plans over to the Hawaii County Building Office and left them to be permitted. And then we waited.

Meanwhile I picked a date based on the projected delivery date of the approved permits (which ironically turned out to be the 14th anniversary of meeting Patrick). I booked my flight and began arrangements to move to Hawaii for the duration of the construction. Patrick didn't intend to come for the building, leaving it up to me to build our house, which in a way was fine—I didn't really fancy having to negotiate the daily details of building with Patrick.

Don's house in Kehena Beach became available for a live-in caregiver to start right about the time I was arriving. Jeff, his former caregiver, was moving back to the mainland. I got my home equity loan of $125,000 approved, which I figured would be just enough to get the house built. Everything seemed to conspire to make this project happen—until the first big hitch.

Patrick and I had one of our infamous meltdowns one Saturday morning. It started out as an argument over the car. He was using my car to get coffee in the morning, but he would never say thank you, wouldn't put gas in the car, and then would complain about something like my use of some of his food to make him dinner. When Patrick is in financial scarcity, there is absolutely no peace in the house. I believe he sensed that this house construction was going to be a big financial liability and he started biting me.

It escalated to the point where I yelled, "I wish you would die in a car accident." He came pretty close to tears and stormed off upstairs to his room. Apparently he had just had a dream that he died in a car crash and it touched a nerve. After a while, I went to his room and apologized and asked if we could go for a walk.

Settling a dispute with Patrick is tricky. First I have to apologize and completely drop whatever issue we were fighting about. Then I have to invite him to do something fun—he's like a child that way.

"Look Sweets, I'm sorry I said those horrible things to you. They were rotten and I'm really sorry. I just got really upset and that's what came out. Why don't we go for a walk?" I asked him in his room after an hour had passed. He grudgingly agreed and put his shoes on. I was pretty sure that I had done some major damage this time and hoped our walk might reveal something. We had some big plans on the table and keeping our relations civil was paramount.

On our walk, I came up with an idea. I suggested to him that he buy into the townhouse in Tucson—he had an extra $100,000 that he had left over from the sale of an old family farm in France. (I've always been stunned by Patrick's ability to come up with large sums of cash in short order and then argue with me over the cost of two ounces of aged cheddar cheese.) We would jointly own the Tucson townhouse, and I would then buy him out of the Hawaii property absolving him of any obligations and rights to the new construction.

The plan took shape: He would stay on in Tucson to look after the place and find work. He had grown weary of San Francisco and was ready for something entirely different and so he agreed to retrieve his furniture and books from the Bay Area on his next trip. I would pay off my loan on the Tucson house and the home equity loan would fund the rest of the Hawaiian construction.

We finished the walk smiling and knowing this was the right plan for both of us. I think he was very relieved not to be facing the untold stresses of house construction. And I was invigorated by the challenge. We also had an investment tied up in all this—the 5th Avenue house in Tucson—the one we had just renovated and sold. In one day we called Deed Day, we signed the sale papers of the 5th Avenue house with the realtor, signed the papers to transfer the Hawaii property to my name only, paid off my loan with Wells Fargo, paid Patrick for his share of the Hawaii property, transferred the deed to the townhouse out of the bank's name to be jointly held by both of us and signed the Wells Fargo home equity loan papers. It was an unbelievable orchestration of events that started at the title company, took us to the county office, the bank, and finally FedEx.

I began assembling six large boxes from the post office in my bedroom. I lined them all up and dropped things in each one to distribute the weight evenly. I packed a mixture of towels, clothes, shoes, office supplies, cooking utensils, a few books, mosquito netting, a raincoat, sun hat, motorcycle helmet (what was I thinking?), sex supplies and a candelabra for fun. I taped up the boxes and dropped them off at the post office in Tucson. They would arrive in six weeks at the Pahoa post office, 17 miles up the hill from Don's house, hopefully all intact.

On my last weekend in Tucson, Patrick planned a going away pool party with a Hawaiian theme. We had reached a new level of peace with each other and this celebration was a very sweet gesture. He invited my friends and made tropical cocktails for us. He wandered about the house shirtless with beads and tropical print shorts, pouring blender drinks, while we played Hawaiian music I had collected over the years. In fact, the very first party Patrick and I ever hosted together was on my birthday in February 1992—a Hawaiian luau held at my apartment in San Francisco. Then we had decorated the Edwardian flat with a giant rented palm tree in the foyer, colored lights, and an erupting volcano cake into which we sacrificed little dolls. We had turned the heat up and dressed in grass skirts purchased at Castro Hardware and done hula performances to an album of vintage Hawaiian music, which we played at the Tucson party 13 years later.

My farewell party really felt like goodbye, with a little fuck-you to Tucson. It was not a "see you later" party. I had given up on Tucson. I simply couldn't make my desert life interesting and fabulous. I had failed at recreating the bling of my California life in Arizona. I had given Tucson four years and figured that was enough. I had only amassed a small handful of friends—not enough to keep me stimulated. I spent most of my weekends by myself watching

Patrick snoring in the chair by the fireplace while I watched PBS documentaries.

At last it was time to go. Scott Rebman, the first person I met when I arrived at the realtor's office in Tucson in 2001, drove me to the airport. Somehow having him be the last one I'd see was perfectly symmetrical—bookending my tenure in the Old Pueblo.

I felt so good to be leaving, though I was a little concerned about leaving Patrick alone in a city where I had failed. Patrick is far less gregarious than I. Being new in town and shy was going to be trouble. I figured at the very least he'd take good care of the house though. And so I headed first to San Francisco with a short layover to see some friends and then on to the big Hawaiian adventure. I had another well-attended sendoff, this time at a restaurant in San Francisco. I think a lot of people have at some point entertained the notion of moving to a tropical island, and so they were eager to see me off on the adventure.

I finally set off over the ocean, bound for that small patch of newly leveled lava. I caught a glimpse of the craggy Farallon Islands, just off the coast of San Francisco, before the sedatives kicked in and I fell asleep. I love taking drugs on airplanes—sitting for hours with my bony knees crammed up against the seat pocket in front of me with some ADHD kid kicking me from behind is magically erased, and I'm transported in a dream to a new place. The inanity of explaining how to exit the airplane in an orderly fashion in the "unlikely event" of a water landing seems to make perfect sense as seen on a couple hits of Xanax. When has there *ever* been a safe and orderly evacuation of a plane after a water landing? Wouldn't I just trample everyone on my way out and use the kid with ADHD as a flotation device?

I awoke in a drugged haze with my head on my neighbor's shoulder. He greeted me with a slightly acerbic, "Morning, honey." He was a big, hairy guy with a beard—the kind you'd see driving a Harley Davidson. I was horrified—I had slept the entire flight with my head perched on his shoulder. Fortunately, he was cool about my limp-necked transgression—at least I didn't fill his breast pocket with drool.

Sheepishly apologizing to the shoulder guy, I deplaned and transferred to the inter-island flight to the Big Island via the terribly un-modern "wiki-wiki" (the blue diesel bus that Patrick calls the kiwi-kiwi), at last arriving in a very rainy Hilo, the nearest airport to my property, shortly after 1 pm on June 5. My new friends Carl Johnson and Bill Fultz, whom I had met on the exploratory trip earlier in the year, met me at the airport. "Aloha! Welcome home," Carl said as he placed a lei of fragrant tuberoses over my head. His words were not lost on me.

We drove through the pouring rain to the small town of Pahoa and stopped for some groceries. Each time I have returned, something new has popped up in this once teeny blip of a town. Now there is a hardware store, Internet café, Subway sandwich shop, fish market, and grocery store. The progress was heartening for me. I didn't fancy having to do a 70-mile roundtrip to Hilo for groceries.

They showed me the new Malama Market—a more upscale grocery store than had ever existed in Pahoa. I was heartened to see it and shocked at the prices: a can of tomato sauce going for $9! Yowza, I'm going to be eating a lot of brown rice, I thought. I bought a bag of groceries for $45, and then we headed down toward the coast.

The 17 mile drive from Pahoa to Seaview crests at the Steam Vents—a popular cruising place for gay men. I imagined I'd be getting to know the Vents well. I had spent some time there on earlier trips. Each time I returned it had become more popular with the burgeoning gay male population in Puna. Cars line the road at the head of the trail through the guava and mango trees to the caves where men meet and steam naked together. It's the closest Puna will likely ever come to having a bathhouse. Fortuitously, a gay man who approves of its current use owns the property.

We dropped Carl off at his house a few miles downhill from the Steam Vents. Carl has a huge piece of land that overlooks the ocean where he built a giant greenhouse. He and his partner actually live in the greenhouse—a bit like the 70s film *Silent Running*. Living in a house with screens for walls presents some interesting challenges like when storms blow the bedding off the bed while they're sleeping. I said goodbye to him and he offered to help with bamboo starts when I got to the point of landscaping my property.

The road heads steadily downhill to the Red Road, which T's off at the lava flow at Kaimu. Incidentally, the Red Road was named as such back when it was a "dirt" road paved with ground-up red lava. It is now paved and no longer red. Calling a black top road the Red Road is just one of the many quirks and incongruities of Puna.

Here at the T there was once a legendary sandy beach with swaying palm trees that was a favorite of surfers. Now it is a vast expanse of black lava all the way to the ocean. Everyone was forced to move their beach-going activities to the tiny Kehena Beach a few miles down the road, where I will be staying.

Bill and I continue along the lava and ohia forest, and quite suddenly the road comes to a deep, dark jungle with tree canopies overhanging the road, cardinals singing, and mangoes, guavas, and avocadoes littering the roadside. It is a sight that takes your breath away, relaxes you with its cool shade and at the same time throws a mysterious dark cloak over you as you enter. All who come to the neighborhood must pass through this ominous gateway. There is an air of darkness to it that is more than just a measure of the light level.

We make the left into Kehena Beach Estates just before the blue tiled Ramashala resort/monastery (is it a resort or is it a monastery?)

and then a quick right onto Kii Nani at the watsu house, then all the way to the end across from the guava trail. There among the thick avocado, monkey pod, and macadamia trees stands my home for the next six months—a slightly rundown and unpainted, two-story pentagonal wooden kit house: Don's funky jungalow with two large lots of lawn to tend to. I scanned the calf-high un-mowed grass awaiting my attention.

The rain had stopped as it often does when you descend from Pahoa. I grabbed my suitcases out of Bill's truck and thanked him for the ride. I noticed Bill looking me over carefully as he helped me to the door. He wasn't "checking me out" so much as checking to see if I was going to be OK in this strange new place. He had left his life as a straight, married lawyer with two kids in Washington, DC to come out and start over as a gay man. He even built his own house in Seaview. Bill, more than anyone, knew *exactly* what I was in for. "Goodbye cutie. And welcome home." He looked back and smiled at me as he got in his truck and gave me a parting glance that I was trying to interpret—was it a "Welcome to the club" or "Oh you poor dear, what have you gotten yourself into?"

I opened up the house, which smelled slightly of mildew by yanking on the door practically to the point of pulling my arm out of socket. The house creaked as I walked across its wooden floors covered with bad 1970s linoleum squares. A piece of gilded bread was nestled in the thrift store chandelier with one working bulb that hung over the long table in the kitchen—the creation of Max (Don's ex-boyfriend). A spider had spun a web bridging the arms of the fixture. The house was full of dirty baby dolls with messy hair in suitcases, bad landscape paintings on which were written Dadaist inanities coming from a deer's mouth like, "Get in the car. What? Get in the car." Kitsch collected at garage sales and the flea markets fills every available nook and shelf.

The house has a playful, wacky feel to it, even if it does seem like it's about to collapse. I have been in the house for a number of earthquakes and perhaps its loose construction allows it to sway with the earth, doing its own hula dance and leaving it standing. Shortly after I moved in however, the upstairs rainwater cistern fell when its rotting wood perch collapsed. The tank hit the roof in the middle of the night scaring the daylights out of me and spilling its 50-gallon payload over the edge, but remarkably, the roof didn't leak.

I opened my suitcase and spilled out my essentials, set up a mosquito net and took a nap, still coming back from the Xanax. I awoke from the nap to the sounds of cardinals warbling in the trees and the afternoon light filtering through lace curtains in Max's room.

It took me a minute to figure out where I was. My eyes scanned the room; I inhaled the fresh and humid air—so thick you can practically chew it. I could smell the plumeria blossoms, the rotting jungle, and the ocean. Sweet, sour, and salty all in one breath. Coming from the thorn forests of the Sonoran Desert of Arizona, it was as if I had gone through some portal into a strange new world without thorns. Indeed I had gone through the looking glass to a moist tropical wonderland. But I was wrong about the thorns.

"Welcome home," I whispered to myself.

Day one.

4

June 27, 2005

OH GOD, WHAT HAVE I DONE?

Day Twenty-Two

Well, after three weeks I'm still waiting for permits. I guess this email will not include time-lapsed photographs of my house erecting itself while I stand idly by, flashing smiles of adoration for the paparazzi. Nope. We're still waiting for a stamp of approval while the one guy at Planning is out sick. You'll get the idea from this installment that I have a lot of spare time.

In the meantime I had an electrician install a temporary power pole on a tripod to the left of the lot. Hawaiian Electric Light Company (appropriately named HELCO) came out and attached it to the power grid, energizing a meter and two plugs. Wow—electricity in the middle of the lava field!

A couple days later, Waterworks sent a guileless young worker named Cody, who worked with his shirt off and spoke softly while installing the water tank at the rear of the lot. Cody is the second contractor I've hired at the house who is a Comparative Literature

major doing construction. And he's the first contractor to show a goodly amount of plumber's crack while working. I snapped a few pictures as he was tightening the tank's bolts while his waistband loosened. We're getting off to a good start.

Cody and his assistant arrived with the curved panels of stainless steel that comprise the sides of the 10,000-gallon water tank that will hold the rainwater collected from the roof to be. This state of the art system will ultimately collect the rain, filter it for particulate matter and then sterilize it with a UV filter until it's perfectly drinkable (as long as you keep rats, birds, slugs, and algae out of the system). After all, it is essentially distilled water. Water will then circulate back to the roof to be heated in a solar panel and stored in a hot water tank inside the house for use as needed. Until then it is basically an expensive above ground swimming pool.

The cesspool is also under way as we have the sanitation engineer's permits to begin. The giant backhoe came squeaking and clacking like a tank across the ferns of the rear adjoining lot one afternoon. It began scooping out a deep hole for the sewage from the house. Unfortunately the sides of the hole caved in and the hole got bigger and bigger and ultimately threatened to take the entire backhoe in with it.

The plan for the cesspool was abandoned, and the workers had to start over by building an interlocking ring of cinder block inside—oh, what's another $1,500? They capped it with ohia logs, poured cement over it, and promptly covered it with the wrong color cinders: red when it should have been maroon. The workers laughed at me when I complained that they delivered the wrong color cinders. I laughed at *them* when they left the cap sitting about two feet higher than the rest of the yard. I made them deliver an extra load of cinders to build up around it so that I wouldn't always have to look at my cesspool mound in the backyard.

It was at this point that I devised a three-part credo for construction that was going to see me through this venture: 1. There's always a solution; 2. It's only money; 3. What's the big hurry? In times of building crises, I repeated this mantra to myself like a Catholic doing ten Hail Marys. I clutched my checkbook like rosary beads and recited it over and over.

The rains have been relentless here the last couple weeks. Towels and clothes have been mildewing at Don's. But the last two days have been beautiful, and I'm reminded of one of the reasons that I moved here—the extraordinary beauty of it all when it's glistening in the sun. The ocean becomes a deep sapphire blue whipped white as it slams into the coast. And then there's the green of the jungle and the undulating black pahoehoe lava.

I spend much of my days running errands in town in Boner (Don and Max's car) like one would do anywhere else. This will soon come to an end soon, as Boner needs new tires and a taillight to pass inspection and I'm not about to spend $600 on someone else's car.

Living here has uncovered some of the nuances that you're likely to miss vacationing in Hawaii. There is a tale of two lands on this island. In this case it's the tale of the dry side versus the wet side: Kona versus Puna. It's a rivalry that amuses those of us squishing around in slug and frog world in the grips of mold and mildew, dutifully composting our vegetable skins and patching our rust bucket cars. We deceive ourselves into thinking we have it better than those *poor suckers* in Kona who tool around the desert-dry side in their rust-free BMWs on their way to brunch at the Hapuna Beach Prince Hotel, the hotel that offers rooms at $7,000 a night.

Grit builds character, I tell myself during sleepless nights in the jungle listening to roaches scrambling through my toiletries looking for a little toothpaste snack. Grit and character—the hallmarks of Puna.

Tourists come here, certainly, but it's a different ilk of vacationer who braves the mold coast. We get the adventure tours, the yogis, the alternative gays, and the Europeans interested in the wildness and getting stoned on the beach. Here they find a world where no one wears deodorant and the women don't shave their legs. We get people who want to sit naked in steam caves, play fetch with dolphins, and walk on lava flows by moonlight. We get the changing room without a curtain at the Jungle Love clothing store in Pahoa, because who really cares if you're seen naked anyway? The police wouldn't come if you called them—if we had them. Puna is a place of outlaws, heretics and anarchists. We even have a few Christians, too, like the couple I met at the beach last week: naked Christians praying they'll find a job but chillin' in the meantime.

No BMWs here. No brunch here. Do we even have a hotel in Puna? Do we even have a beach? Kehena Beach is more like a temporary gathering of black sand where the cliffs meet the sea, beautiful but disappearing with the rising sea and sinking land.

I have moments when I question why I came here. Perhaps I find Island life appealing because I watched too many episodes of *Gilligan's Island* as a child. Which of the castaways have I become—Gilligan or is it Ginger? (Really, I wanted to be Mrs. Thurston Howell, III.) To see some of the contraptions people invent here, it seems that we were all watching the same TV show—like the woman in Seaview with the single photo-voltaic panel attached to a car battery and one small light bulb with which to read by. I imagine that Mary Ann is out back pumping away on a bicycle generator on the days without sunshine. Then there's the guy in Seaview who uses successive Rubbermaid tubs strung together with hoses to catch rainwater. The Professor would undoubtedly be lecturing him on the ills of the dreaded rat lung disease that could infest his untreated water.

Then there's my own climbing to the highest point of the property, standing on tippy-toes and holding the cell phone up in the air with the antenna extended and pointed around a cinder cone in order to make a phone call; or when I have to park Boner in the middle of Don's street with a sign on the windshield that has the house address on it hoping FedEx will find the house which doesn't appear in their corporate computer. These are the moments when I think, What in God's name have I done? I've gone too far this time. I'm living on a remote island jungle where the houses are off the grid, people are off their rockers, and fruit flies are eager to convert my dinner scraps into their maggoty birthing center.

The property values here continue to rise without any sign of gravity. Real estate speculators will buy a piece of property here, double its purchase price and park it on the market to see if some sucker from California or Maui will buy it. And yes, they will. There is talk about the bubble bursting, much like the talk in the Bay Area five years ago when no one thought that property would go up any more after the dot-com crash. In five years, properties in the Bay Area tripled in value from their already exorbitantly high levels.

Nature has a way of righting things, though. Like earthquakes in California, the reality of living on an active volcano is that one day we may become the modern-day Pompeii. People in Puna will be preserved in lava for eternity in their yurts and junked school buses lighting up a joint or fixing the old Puna ride.

Mauna Loa is expected to blow any time now ("now" being used in geological time). The earth near its caldera has been trembling like the mouth of an old woman about to speak. Hawaii's biggest active volcano is a shield volcano, so she likely won't explode like Krakatoa, but she is expected to drool enough lava in one hour to pave a 4-foot sidewalk from here to New York (if only we had a sidewalk to New York). Last time it erupted (1984), the lava came within a mile of Hilo. Mauna Loa, scientists say, doesn't pose the threat to coastal Puna that Kilauea does.

Scientific opinion tends to differ from the "pakalolo" (*crazy weed:* marijuana) induced prognostications that you often hear in Puna, and this time, scientists opine that Mauna Loa will likely flow to the other side of the island and reach Kona. Always the opportunist, I thought maybe after a lava flow I will be able to afford to live in sunny Kona.

Lots here in Puna that were next to the 1989 lava flow from Kilauea were reduced in value to $100. These lots are now worth $150,000. So you can see how land ownership on this side of the island, on the slopes of Kilauea (the most active volcano on earth) can be a wild ride. Puna is a place of tall tales, land speculation, and geological oddities. One day you can be basking in your tropical idyll and wake up to find lava spouting out of the ground near your house. This happened in 1960 when the town of Kapoho literally split in two along a fault and a lava fountain spouted like a red-hot whale in the middle of a field.

Thus the real estate market is one in which you can lose your aloha shirt—where one day a princess becomes a pauper. It can happen by sea with tsunamis or by land with lava or by air with hurricanes. In short, Puna is not for the effete, the faint of heart and is no place for a sissy. So why are gay folks moving here en masse? Anywhere else in rural America gays are nearly invisible but not so here. A visit to Malama Market in Pahoa often turns up congregations of dykes and queens in the aisles trading building tips and gossip.

How did this happen? Must we colonize dangerous lands for the thrill of it, or is it that we give makeovers to beautiful places in need of a little attention? Or is it that we like to live at the ends of the world—in remote places for safety from our straight oppressors? Provincetown, Fire Island, Key West—all hard to get to, out of the way—the last place you'd expect to find a colony of homos. Add

Puna to the list. Coming out of the ashes of Kilauea's devastating lava flow, the Puna coast of the Big Island of Hawaii is destined for an extreme makeover and like they saw the devastating lava coming, the locals see the gays as yet another encroachment on their fragile world.

Tensions between queers and straights erupt from time to time at Kehena Beach or in Pahoa. In fact, Puna was the first place I have ever been gay bashed. One afternoon this week I sat half way down the rocky cliffs of Kehena watching the ocean and suddenly felt a sharp whack on my back. I looked up to the top of the cliff to see a group of local teenage boys darting through the woods. On instinct, I chased after them and confronted them demanding to know who threw the rock. My ire intimidated them and no one confessed. I could see they were a bunch of scared kids who thought they could get away with attacking the gay haole. I got their license plate number and stormed up the guava trail to call it in to the police who apparently knew the family and went to their house to apprehend them. Of course, I had no proof and wasn't seriously hurt, so nothing came of this. I wondered if this was an inauspicious beginning to my new Hawaiian chapter.

However, I squawked loudly and the local gay population answered the call with the first-ever Kehena Beach Gay Pride Day. Richard from Kalani Honua (the gay-owned retreat center down the Red Road) put the word out that we in Puna would not stand for violence in our community. His message went out on the "coconut wireless" (the rumor mill) that we would gather at the beach on Sunday in solidarity. About 15 men showed up for a naked beach picnic to celebrate gay pride. As a newcomer, I felt a little self-conscious to be the impetus for this event but realized that it had been coming for a while. A couple of men sat on the beach and showed me their pellet gun scars from previous homophobic (or nude-phobic) potshots taken at them from atop the cliffs.

Any event at Kehena beach is, de facto, a nude affair and Gay Pride was no exception. Although nudity is technically illegal in the state of Hawaii, it goes un-enforced at Kehena. I think the state officials are either too understaffed or rightfully scared of a band of naked hippies charging them if they were ever to show up to arrest anyone. So they look the other way and accommodate yet another transgression of the invasive white folk.

While a man was showing me his pellet wounds, a sexy, youngish guy showed up on the beach, immediately exchanging smiles with me. Spellbound by his creamy brown skin, black hair and brown eyes (my favorite color scheme in a man) I couldn't contain my arousal. I had strayed from my blanket naked and had nothing to cover up my burgeoning admiration of his beauty. Of course, he couldn't help noticing and he came closer and introduced himself. He was still clothed but I noticed a lump had appeared in his pants as a response to my erection. Ah, the beginning of a non-verbal conversation. An erect penis puts out a very clear message—if you can't win someone over conversationally, why not just let the equipment do the talking? It is after all, doing the thinking. A little wet spot appeared at the end of the lump in his pants, which hastened our non-verbal conversation to the inevitable conclusion: it was time to depart this beach-bound Gay Pride for a few minutes. We climbed the cliffs on all threes and ended up in a passionate hour of sex at Don's house. He was slightly stinky with an uncircumcised and un-deodorized, natural body odor (yum) and tasted like pot smoke (bah). We returned to the beach all smiles, dirty, and sweaty—nothing that a little dip in the ocean couldn't repair.

Was *this* the auspicious beginning of my new life that I was hoping for? I was confused by the conflicting messages of homophobia and eros at Kehena Beach. And the waiting continues.

Love, Seaweed

5

July 7, 2005

WE HAVE SLAB

Day Thirty-Two

After weeks of my calling to schedule and re-schedule the work and finally an ultimatum to get it done or I would be switching contractors, the hunky Scott Gebbe finally called one afternoon to say, "We'll be there at 6 am tomorrow." In preparation, I measured the lot by foot and eyeballed the distance that the house should sit from the street. And then I got out my spray paint and drew bright pink lines on the lava where the front edge of the slab would start.

Scott arrived before dawn, confident and bold as a swashbuckler accompanied by his pirates. As one of the only decent concrete workers in Puna, he knows he has a lot of power over owner-builders who salivate for his perfect work even if he delays you almost to the point of cancellation. That's part of the appeal for contractors—to have a reputation that makes clients beg for them and then you'll submit and willingly pay any price. And with any contractor of merit in this Hawaiian building frenzy, they get to you when they're good and ready and you'll be grateful they showed up. I have learned now that you can't ask too many questions—just grab your checkbook and get the hell out of the way. And so I did.

Scott oversaw the building of the forms that would hold the wet cement, and then we waited for the base coarse delivery that lines the bed before the cement is poured. I filmed the first piece of rebar going into the ground with a steely *whack* of a sledgehammer. The cornerstone had been laid.

Then came the pouring. I stood at the lot at dawn on the day of delivery waiting and listening for the roar of the cement truck coming up the main road. It arrived right on schedule … and kept right on going. Crap. The truck continued on past the site and disappeared from view. Out here without cell phones or radio signal, this could be trouble. He might never come back and without cement I'd lose my precious appointment with Scott. I scrambled to find the keys to Boner to chase down the lost truck and lead them back to the property.

Fortunately they had not gone too far and I was able to catch up with them. The cement truck dumped its lumpy gray payload into the forms while I watched like Marlin Perkins from a "safe distance." I couldn't help noticing that Scott took his shirt off—was this for my benefit? Perhaps I was getting my money's worth *now*. Surely he knows that he's hunky with his bulging biceps and hairy chest glistening in the morning rain. And he kept calling me "handsome." He is married with child but recognizes that it's mostly gay men building here, and showing off his gym-toned chest and flirting a little is undoubtedly good for business. The message of metro-sexuality—mostly a mainland concept—seems to have made it to him.

After hours of running a gas-powered polishing device called "the bird" on the wet surface, Scott wrought the surface to the point that I could actually see my reflection, assuring me it would look like marble in the end. When he was done, I saw the blue of the sky and the clouds reflected in its surface.

Seeing the slab poured was an emotional process that caught me by surprise. There's no denying now that there will be a structure on a solid foundation built to last at least a few lifetimes. It is predicted that thousands of years from now, the island will collapse under its own weight, tearing it all asunder. Short of a premature collapse or a lava flow, this slab will be there through fire, hurricane, and earthquake.

The permanence of my mark on this land struck me. Nothing I had done heretofore had that sense of indelibility, and up until now, I could have turned back. This house is to be a place of my own, designed to be the stage for the second half of my life. Friends, family, lovers, people I have yet to meet and people I will never know, will come and go on this floor. Love, fighting, dancing, meals, retching, will all occur on this floor. One day I may very well die on this floor, in this house, in this field of knee-high orchids.

After the crew left, with the strong afternoon trade winds whistling across the lava and through the one native tree, I dreamed of the romantic promise of this house and yet felt the stinging loneliness of carving a single name into the foundation with a loose nail. Facing the ocean on the western side, I unceremoniously scratched out the letters in my best cursive: "Seaweed '05."

The foundation stands now, amid a fern prairie on the side of a volcano on this remote and wild island. The whole process of beginning construction was so overwhelming that I went back to Don's house, crawled into bed and pulled pillows over my head.

When the slab hardens, I thought, I'll go over and have a little dance party on it to celebrate. There won't be a whole lot of time in which to do it—the first floor lumber drop arrives Thursday and shortly thereafter the framing begins. I'm told it will go up fast now.

Joe

On another note, this week I met a lively, smart guy named Joe who is a volunteer at Kalani. He sports a shock of bleach blond hair and precious eyeglasses—artifice that confirms that Joe, though not blessed with a generous amount of natural good looks, has done the best he can. These are the visual markers of a well put-together homosexual—something endearing to me in a place full of gorgeous straight men who waste their gifts of natural beauty by wearing crappy, dirty clothes and taking that just-out-of-bed look to the streets. Joe is one of those men who would never go out with his hair sticking up or crumbs clinging to the corners of his mouth.

Being a volunteer at Kalani means that he pays a fee and does either landscaping or housekeeping in exchange for meals and lodging. Joe and I smiled at each other one evening sucking down the wine at a reception for some event where we really should have been more participatory. Instead, we just went for the free wine. We stood at the side table as people kicked off their shoes and moved onto the dance floor for some welcoming ritual for a group of volunteers.

"I guess you're not into the ritual, huh?" I asked.

His face lit up and he came closer with his eyes rolling. Wiggling his head and body, he said under his breath, "Are you kidding? I'm not into this new age shit." He burst out laughing and tossed back the wine. His irreverence made me laugh and we hoisted another plastic cup of cheap wine together and watched the women whirling about in diaphanous sarongs to world beat music that seemed so terribly 1990s.

Joe showed me his pocketful of Klonopin for those tense nights of being a middle-aged lawyer from Boston in a jungle full of 20-somethings experimenting with sex and drugs and living away from home for the first time. I could relate. I knew he wouldn't last long at Kalani.

As I predicted, Joe went AWOL from Kalani after three weeks, cutting short his agreement. He moved in to the guest room at Don's house for a week. We slipped off for an adventure to Volcanoes National Park and the Wood Valley Temple, a Buddhist retreat center in Pahala. Joe was trying to be more reverent, though failing miserably. He preferred the gift shop to sitting in silence in the temple—my kind of guy.

We sat outside at a picnic table feeding the peacocks and giggling. "Did you hear that?" I asked dropping another chip on the ground for the ridiculously beautiful bird.

"What?"

"The farting noise? I think the Rinpoche farted," I said.

"No he didn't. Rinpoches don't fart … Ow!" An aggresive peacock bit his hand while he was feeding it.

"He did. I heard it. It was a distinct fart. I think he even rang a bell to cover it up." I volleyed back.

"I'm not feeding this fucking bird. It's nothing more than a fucking blue chicken. He bit my hand!" He pouted and smiled at the same time.

I was so delighted to have met someone who would be so irreverent as to swear at a temple calling a sacred peacock a "fucking blue chicken." We joked about what barbecued peacock and a peacock omelet would taste like. Hawaii was causing us both to lose our mainland sense of decorum.

Joe and I took another trip to the south side of the island to the Green Sand Beach while I waited for the next stage of construction to begin. We hiked along the orange dirt cliffs toward the beach laughing and gossiping about all the weirdoes in Puna and yet noticing how freeing it was to be off the mainland grid of propriety for a while. We arrived at the beach and Joe realized he had forgotten his bathing suit. So in the spirit of irreverence, and knowing we were out of reach of the police, we both shucked our shorts and went body surfing naked in the warm waves.

Joe helped me learn one painful lesson about friendships and relationships in Hawaii: no matter how well you connect, no matter how hot you might be for each other, nearly everyone eventually returns to their lives on the mainland. You may have a lovely night making love on a cliff overlooking the ocean under the moon with only the whales as your witness. But you'll inevitably be taking them to the airport in a few days waving goodbye to them as they head off to security with flowers around their neck. You'll remain in their memories as the exotic adventurer on that steamy island. There will be a follow up phone call and then the emails will trail off over time. They will tame their wildness as they re-enter their urban lives and you'll probably never see or hear from them again.

So I enjoyed my moment in the surf with Joe and the bitter sweetness of knowing he would leave soon and return to his boyfriend in Boston. I wondered what sort of detached monster I would become in such a transient place.

Oh, and the sand is indeed green: olive with gold speckles.

Love, Seaweed

6

July 17, 2005

BONER'S LAST RIDE

Day Forty-Two

Week six was the week Boner and I parted company. Boner, Max and Don's 15-year-old car I was using, broke down three times with a rusted radiator that required me to stop and refill it with water about every ten miles. One night driving home from the airport with my friend Richard, who just arrived from San Francisco, the car started to overheat so we pulled off the Red Road only about a mile from home, opened the hood and waited for it to cool to finish the trip to Don's house.

Julie, a bouncy, blonde woman with very large breasts (whom I know from the beach as "Julie with the Boobs"), happened to be driving by and slowed her Jeep to offer help.

"Do ya'll need any help?" she asked in a Valley Girl accent. I couldn't see her face in the dark but I knew who she was by her Jeep. I was sure her hair and tits were bouncing as she spoke.

"Have you got a flashlight?" I yelled back to her from inside Boner.

"No, but I have sparklers!" she giggled.

I looked at Richard and we both laughed. This is the essence of Puna—goofing off in the face of adversity. In this moment, short of a tow truck and a hunky mechanic to rescue us, a little comic relief was just what we needed, and Julie with the Boobs provided it. She jumped out of her Jeep and produced a lighter and lit up three sparklers. There we all stood in the middle of the Red Road, in the pitch darkness, twirling sparklers and laughing. When our sparklers burned out, we added water to the radiator and made the final stretch home.

The next day I had Boner towed eight miles up hill to the mechanic who fixed the cooling system but pronounced the car in danger of breaking in two from a rusted chassis. Rather than face the eventuality of one day witnessing the back half of Boner disappear with my huli chicken and case of Corona in the trunk, I went car shopping immediately.

I am now certain that used car dealers in Hawaii work in concert with the new car dealers. Essentially it's a good cop/bad cop routine: you go to the scariest, neediest, used car dealers you've ever met, and they frighten you all the way over to the new car dealers whereupon you will be comforted with bottles of water and air conditioned lobbies with waxed floors and the soothing strains of slack-key guitar. It's undoubtedly a nepotistic relationship that results in more new car sales.

My used car buying adventure culminated at Aloha Used Cars where Howard the Hawaiian showed me a blue '93 Honda Civic hatchback—exactly what I was looking for. I think "aloha" is one of those words that can have great meaning and yet can mean nothing at all. It is like "love." I take both words with a more prudent skepticism now. A big smile and an emphatic aloha in the used car business means that you're about to get a good bamboozling, so beware.

Anyway, after a couple weeks of looking I was so excited to at last find the right car. Howard and I jumped into the Honda to take it for a little spin. The car, bought in an auction for resale (which I later learned was how most used cars come to the island), was undoubtedly seized after a high-speed chase that involved running over curbs and medians, because the car had a severe pull to the right.

I pointed this out to Howard who said in his pidgin accent, "No man, dere's no drift. Da tyuhs need air, brah. We gon just pull into da gas station and add air wenfo da tyuh."

OK, I thought, perhaps it's the tire pressure—a little low on the right side could be giving it a drift. We pulled in and he proceeded to put air in the tire. Holding the hose to the stem, he clicks off 30 pounds. 40 pounds. 50 pounds. 60 pounds. I start backing away from a tire about to explode. 65 pounds. The car is getting taller and taller.

"Hey Howard," I shouted and winced from about ten feet back, "Don't you think you should check how much pressure the tire needs, first?"

"Oh no problem, brah. It just need air." He didn't seem to get my point.

"Well, you're about to blow the tire up, dude." I stepped up and pushed my fingernail into the stem to release the excess 33 pounds of air while he watched. I realized I needed to assume the role of alpha customer because clearly this guy knows nothing about cars. I wondered not so much where they get these cars, but where they get these car *dealers.*

We got back in the car, and then the "check engine" light came on accompanied by the distinct smell of oil smoke from under the hood. A real beaut this car is, I thought. He says, "No worries brah, dey just spill a little oil on da kine, uh, da kine, uh da block wenfo dey change da oil."

Maybe—it was possible. Howard still denied that there was any drift to the steering, so I let go of the wheel while we were arguing and let the car careen off the road until he quickly grabbed it and steered it back onto the road. I think this illustrated my point pretty clearly. He shut up—my case having been made with the potential loss of his life.

It's at this point I noticed the odometer had been disconnected. This car probably has 500,000 miles on it and was used as a taxicab in Honolulu. I thought, OK, that's it, Mister—I'm done. I let the car steer itself back to the dealership as it was all right turns from where we were and quickly I slipped out of the car and into the truck where my friend Chris was waiting for me. I locked the door quickly. "Let's get outta here, Chris," I muttered under my breath hoping Howard couldn't read lips.

Howard starts approaching the car, "Brah—make me an offer!" The car's asking price as written on the windshield was $4,950. He reduced it on the spot to $3,000. Then $2,500.

"How about $2,000? Just make an offer, my friend." Now he's stalking us as Chris has thrown his truck into reverse and I'm quickly rolling up the window on Howard's very desperate pleas to make him any reasonable offer.

"Wait I gon talk to my boss!" Howard is grabbing at the moving truck as if he was going to stick his fingers in the closing window preventing us from leaving.

What is it with that "boss" thing? It seems to be a universality of car-buying—that your dealer will have to talk to the shifty-eyed boss smoking cigars in a pinstriped suit in some glass booth in the back of the showroom. Somehow you feel more powerful that your dealer has had to confer with the Big Guy to accommodate you, and that the Big Guy could very well come after you should you skate on the deal. Shouldn't car dealers be empowered to make their own deals already knowing what their bottom line is?

Traumatized by this attempt to buy a used car, Chris and I raced to the new Toyota dealership. I'm sorry; I admit that I'm hopelessly suburban. I wanted to be treated with respect and handed a nice little packet of information, a checklist, and a warranty. I wanted that new car smell instead of some cheesy new car scent sprayed all over the interior of what was clearly a stinky dog's car.

That afternoon, I bought a new 2005 Toyota Scion. Yes, it looks like a toaster on wheels. And it gets 37 miles to the gallon and has a warranty. It came with tinted windows, MP3 player, and airbags—all the modern refinements that my life thus far has been severely lacking. At least when I'm in the car, there will be a sense of order in this chaotic time. This car is 15 years newer than my mainland car, though it gets about the same gas mileage as my 1990 Honda Civic in Tucson.

I returned to the jungalow in the new car, pulling it up to the house away from potentially falling coconuts. I opened the garage and cleared some space for the new car and drove it in. In a stroke of insect paranoia, I poured a moat of boric acid around the car and put roach traps under the seats. If a roach was going to walk into the car, it was going to meet with an itchy and desiccating death in the powder surrounding the car. All I had to do was cover the tracks up each time I returned it safely to the center of the ring.

That weekend I took a little trip to the dry side of the island to go snorkeling. It was great not to have to stop every ten miles to check the coolant and add water. This time, the Kona trip delivered not only respite from the jungle but a sense that I had indeed chosen the correct side of the island to build a life. Kona was crawling with overweight rich people looking for salt-water taffy and feeding their bratty kids junk food. We couldn't find a single decent radio station until we came back across the lava fields of Volcanoes National Park and picked up Hawaiian Public Radio from Hilo.

Snorkeling has become a new passion—it's like flying without an airplane. I imagine myself soaring over cliffs and valleys as I glide over coral and rocks. It's kind of a cheap thrill and a chance to enter a completely different world.

The fish I saw snorkeling were unbelievably luminous—a stunning array of circus colors so whimsically applied to fish scales. I also had the chance to swim with "honu" (green sea turtles) for the first time. I was amazed how unafraid they were of my presence. I followed the swimming dinosaurs around the coral reef just watching with my hands behind my back, kicking slowly with my fins as they nibbled on rocks and surfaced for air every few minutes.

It becomes really clear while snorkeling in Hawaii, why so many tacky paintings attempt to recreate the colors of the fish. If you describe them it does not seem credible: "And then we saw one that had pink polka dots, teal stripes and a big pouty mouth with buck teeth and was eating coral … and then one had a long yellow dorsal fin and a fake eye near the tail that made it look like it was swimming backwards." It's easier just to paint them. I promised to stop making fun of fish art and fish t-shirts.

My favorite fish is actually the Hawaiian state fish: the humumu-nukunuku-apua'a, which if you can say without stopping, gives you tacit permission to live in Hawaii. For those who just can't say it, it is called the Picasso Triggerfish. It looks like a bug-eyed space ship that collided with a pile of butterscotch pudding. Oh, I give up—you'll just have to look it up.

On the home front, we're still waiting for building permits. The house framing begins as soon as we get them. I'm hoping that my builders will not have taken a job by the time I'm ready for them. One of the great challenges of building is the timing—the first floor building supplies are due for delivery tomorrow. The roof trusses arrive on the 11th of August and I still don't have the permits to start.

I ordered several dump trucks of maroon cinders (finely ground lava) to be delivered to the property and had them spread around the slab by the virtuosic Bobcat operator, Duane. I narrowly escaped being run over a few times as I leapt to safety on the slab, stunned by his speed. He shaped a circular driveway around the island that the bulldozers created for the front garden.

Then I purchased a car canopy and installed it myself in the howling wind so that the framers would have a dry place to work, store lumber, and rest. The wind kept pulling the structure over before I could get two poles in. It would have made for a very comic scene, had anyone been watching.

And we just wait and wait.

Love, Seaweed

7

August 3, 2005

MURDER IN THE JUNGLE

Day Fifty-Nine

Construction is still on hold awaiting permits from the county. Each week I call my draftsman to check on the status, and each week they tell me the same thing: next week, next week, next week. I dropped by the slab at the all too quiet construction site just to check on it from time to time. I have begun to wonder if they lost my plans or if this is just going to turn into some horrible third-world experience where I'll never get permits and maybe I need to go down to Hilo and start bribing officials with gift bottles of booze.

So I spent another week going to the beach, reading about Hawaiian history in Queen Liliuokalani's biography and exploring the island and some of Puna's local characters.

Bud

"When you live in the jungle, you learn how to murder." So says Bud, the heavily tattooed groundskeeper from Kalani Honua who whirls around the resort's 19 acres in a tractor, taming the fields of cane grass. He flashes a wicked grin at me as I drive by watching him aggressively carve up the field as if he were driving a combine in a field of corn. He wears big, thick glasses and looks like a Vietnam vet, sweaty and bouncing on the tractor's seat. Mowing that field is his very own grassy *Apocalypse Now*—a war waged on wildness. Bud, by the way, is a homosexual—an incidental and inconsequential detail of this story.

I met Bud lounging naked at the pool. He's one of those people who really should just keep his clothes on or deploy some serious bronzer. He makes no effort to wear sunscreen when he's working under the tropical sun and so when naked, his legs from mid-thigh down and his arms from mid-bicep down look as if they were dipped in a fryer and the rest of his body is pale white. The overall effect when he's seen naked is that of very dark person wearing a white, one-piece woman's bathing suit—a most unfortunate tan line. His back is completely covered in a dark blue-green tattoo—the color that must come loaded in the artist's needle unless you request something nicer. It's a tangle of a tattoo—a jungle drawn out over his entire backside that creeps around his sides to the front and over his shoulders and down his arms. It is a perfect depiction of the surrounding jungles of Puna. If you were to stand still in the jungle, that is exactly what you'd look like within a few days.

Bud delivered his remark about learning how to murder in his droning voice, slightly slurred with no pauses between words, as if some articulation synapses died after a few too many pakalolo tokes. I thought to myself, "Oh dear, this dude is nuts." Well, it turns out he's right and so was I. Tonight I learned that murder is indeed the unwritten law of the jungle and although at first, Bud's elevator didn't appear to be accessing the upper floors, his insanity made perfect sense.

I came to Hawaii to live in a beautiful place by the ocean with friendly gay people. I didn't really come for any love of the jungle itself. Honestly, I prefer the desert. Not having bargained for jungle life, I hadn't planned on a full body hug with the creepy crawlies and tangles of vines that loop themselves in slow motion around your ankles and pull you in. I have definitely been feeling like a desert boy at somewhat of a loss in the jungle. Embracing things has never really been my forté. I'm much more of a *take-my-culture-with-me-and-alter-what-I-cannot-accept* kind of guy. I abide by a reverse serenity prayer of *change the things I cannot accept and complain about the rest.* It's a wonder I'm not an alcoholic—I've been walking the twelve steps backwards for a very long time now.

However, since I arrived, the jungle has been wearing down my resistance, even charming me a bit. With a newfound insouciance, I find myself casually flicking earwigs off my leg with one hand and elegantly squashing them with my flip-flop while dining or talking on the phone and not missing a beat of conversation. The pinchy little bug goes flying with its back arched trying to avenge the swat upon landing. I have even become cavalier about roaches, sometimes just letting them nibble on that dead millipede on the counter top. Hey, everyone has to raid the kitchen for a midnight snack once in a while, and since I'm not really into munching things with a thousand legs, why not share? At least I won't have to clean up the carcass, is my thinking.

There's a way in which the beauty of the jungle has started to emerge. It's about the recycling of life. In California you recycle your Pinot Noir bottles. Here you recycle flesh. Toss a chicken part out the window of your jungalow, and you'll soon see what I mean. Count the minutes until the ants in their little chop shops have managed to strip it to bones. And then, miraculously, even the bones are gone in short order. It's like a car left on the freeway in Los Angeles—stripped to the chassis in just a few days.

Coqui Frogs

I've been curious about that freaky noise in the dark of the jungle that I've been hearing every night? *Toot tweet, toot tweet*—a shrill note and its high octave whistled from some slimy bellows. Repeated again and again and then echoed back from several other places in the jungle. One can hear a deafening chorus of them upon arrival in Puna. This is no forest bird.

Meet the coqui frog. Pronounced like Cokie Roberts, the NPR correspondent. The Coqui is a non-native invasive (isn't everything in Hawaii?) introduced from its native Puerto Rico. The first frogs allegedly hitched a ride several years ago on containers bound for the Home Depot and Walmart in Hilo.

Saying their name produces the sound that the male frog emits all night long at 90+ decibels. It's basically one cubic inch of screaming onomatopoeic hell. The little brown monsters have been known to reproduce like polygamous Mormons—80,000 frogs per acre churning out the eggs. They have evolved to the point that they don't even require standing water in which to lay eggs like other frogs.

The males climb up trees at night and blast away with their whistling noises attracting the females. It's fine if you have two or three in the neighbor's jungle, but when they're outside *your* bedroom, there is no sleeping. Coquis have even been known to induce insanity—you can't get the sound out of your head, and your ears ring even after you've moved to quieter grounds. I visited a friend in the upper reaches of Kalani's jungle and could not hear her talking to me across the table over the frogs' cries.

In Puerto Rico, there are predators like snakes and lizards that Hawaii doesn't have (yet) to keep them in check. Environmental toxins and density of human population have also kept the coqui population at bay in Puerto Rico. Biological balance in Hawaii comes in the form of neighborhood organizations to quell the noisy invasion by killing frogs. I joined a frog lynch mob tonight at a neighbor's house in Kehena Beach. Heretofore, I had never seen one of the little frogs, though I had certainly heard them getting closer to Don's house over the months. After a lecture from a county official about eradication devices, citric acid sprays, and hydrated lime drenches, we waited for the sun to go down. And then we listened quietly from a neighbor's lanai for the first chirps of the evening.

A neighborhood gathering in Kehena Beach means 50% are going to be gay men and the rest aging hippies with names like Mauve and Jade. Odd bedfellows, but aligned in our pursuit of a good night's sleep, we set out into the jungle lots of Kehena Beach Estates armed with flashlights and buckets of citric acid. I was a little wary of this frog murdering business, considering I grew up with Kermit the Frog as my pencil-wristed hero. But the onslaught of the frogs encroaching on my peaceful night's sleep was impetus enough to get me out there with a spray gun.

The way you locate them is to listen and imitate their call with a whistle. They'll call back to you thinking you're another frog, and then you quietly and slowly zero in on them in the dark. You shine the light on their little Louis Armstrong faces all puffed out and blowing, and you either grab 'em with your hand or you zap 'em with the spray. I hate to think what the spray must feel like on their sensitive skin. (Some things are better left un-thought.)

Remarkably, the hippies, the women, the gay people—typically sensitive as we are—were out there en masse. None of the 30 people combing the jungles questioned the humaneness of burning the skin off the poor little creatures. Imagine if someone dipped your most sensitive skin in acid.

This is where Bud's words come in handy. Murder: it's part of jungle life, and no one said a coqui expedition was going to be a pleasant affair. This was also the moment when I made the mistake of looking down at the ground with my flashlight. Murder indeed. I was standing in a pile of writhing slugs and millipedes. Just then a slug dropped out of the tree onto my black cashmere sweater like you'd imagine a python in the Amazon would drop to startle its prey. (Excuse me, what would inspire a slug to just drop out of a tree? Boredom? Tired of going so slow, I think I'll just jump, now?) I freaked out and bolted out to the street patting all parts of myself to make sure I wasn't carrying any stinging insects, and I scraped my shoes on the pavement to get off any remaining slug residue. All this carnage and slime forced me once again to go to my happy place.

Come on, I thought, be a man! Those women and sissies are all in there squashing frogs with their bare hands. Somehow, Arizona with its rattle snakes and cactus spines seemed like child's play compared to the mysterious dank jungle of slimy critters. I mean, earlier today I turned the compost pile and I actually heard thousands of grubs in there churning through the papaya skins, loud and clear. I could actually *listen* to the compost pile. Listen to Bud is what I wanted to do. Murder … murder … murder. Be a man, be a *Hawaiian,* dammit, and go in there and kill something.

So I did. I used my bionic hearing—you know, the ears that got me into dog court suing all my neighbors in Tucson for their barkers. As it turned out, I found more frogs than anyone tonight. I found the first one and the second one. In total, I found five of them, when 30 coquistadors only found a couple frogs. They were nestled in the crevices of palm trees, in the center of big leaves using the foliage to amplify their calls out into the jungle. I spotted one and yelled out to someone to come and grab it. I couldn't bring myself to actually touch one with my bare hands. A butch lesbian named Donna came in and grabbed it and threw it into her zip lock baggie that would be its coffin. That was one less toot tweet in the jungle—now, only 79,999 to go. I found another one—Phil came in with his sprayer. The citric acid hit the frog and it immediately jumped off the leaf taking shelter in the ground cover below. Talk about acid rain. The jungle was getting quieter with each spray and splat. We could hear the sound of the ocean and the delicate rain drops on leaves once again. The soft hum of crickets in the ferns was restored. I imagined how quiet the old Hawaii must have been.

The baggies go in the freezer, I was told—a painless death for the frog. I wished the frog to return soon as something else—to come back next time in Puerto Rico where snakes will keep your population in check.

I lay in bed that night (after carefully scrubbing sticky slug slime off my cashmere sweater) listening to the sound of the surf instead of the frogs for the first time since their invasion. But I was spooked by the thought of the little guys in the freezer who were undoubtedly wondering what in hell had happened to them—their promised land suddenly turned so cold. The next morning I slowly opened the fridge and peered in to see the horror of frozen frogs with their bug-eyes frosted over. Their once brown supple bodies had turned into pale gray frogsickles.

Bud's words gave me courage.

Love, Seaweed

8

August 7, 2005

BUGGED, BOTHERED, AND BEWILDERED

Day Sixty-Three

I have a special announcement: At long last we have building permits and construction begins Friday. The moment I've been waiting months for has finally arrived, but I am too shaken up to care.

I'm recovering from bug hell day. In the two months that I've been here, I've been more than a little tormented by the critters. Actually, it's much worse than that: I think I've become a bug magnet. Bugs seek me out now to terrify me. They know there's a newbie in town, and they can extract maximum fright value out of me.

First it was the maggots in the trash that disappeared my chicken carcass. I had thrown the earthly remains of my huli chicken in the outdoor garbage can like a good suburban boy, first wrapping it in plastic and making sure that the lid was tightly sealed. Several days later I went to throw away the trash and I opened the trashcan to drop my bag in. My first thought was, "Oh, who stuccoed the inside of the trash can? What a lovely pattern." Then I saw that the stucco was moving and the patterns were changing. *Dear Jesus.* Fruit fly maggots had completely coated the inside of the barrel giving it the appearance of a nice antique white stucco finish. I almost vomited all over the trashcan. I made some sort of guttural noise and slammed it shut quickly locating the happy place in my mind: I had to envision rainbows, butterflies, and treacle tarts. Getting to your happy place in a hurry is a very useful skill here in the jungle where you share your life with a seething underworld of flesh-recyclers.

Then it was Frankenroach that I stepped on, squishing its white guts out, and it *still* chased me squealing around the living room. Then it was the evil earwig in the sink that I split into two and the front end came after me to avenge its unfortunate bifurcation on behalf of the back end.

Then I closed the window on a gecko. I was pushing and heaving on the window and grumbling, "Gee, why won't this window close?" Then I saw the delirious little green gecko with a bloody, squashed head, one eye popped out and a broken neck pressed into the L-shape of the window frame. It was looking at me having its last thought, "Dude, did you have to do that? Did you *have* to push on the window?" The ants began eating the dead gecko within minutes.

OK, a gecko is not a bug, but still. So I put on my Irish lament music because I sincerely felt bad for giving some friendly green lizard a horrible and painful death. Besides, they're cute and they eat bugs … and leave stinky little cone-shaped doodies that are basically digested bug carcasses on my pillows. Nonetheless, I was grieving about the poor little gecko with the broken neck.

Although I stopped driving Boner the car, I had to take him to Pahoa for an inspection. While I'm driving I notice a couple ants crawling on the dashboard. No cause for alarm. I don't really despise ants—on the contrary—I think ants are pretty cool when they're not running up my ankles. They carry away the things you don't really want lying around the house—bug carcasses, pieces of meat, boogers dropped behind the sofa. Honestly, I was just starting to get into the symbiosis of life in a place with such a strong insect presence. I don't even mind the mosquitoes so much—they're clean and surgical, and low on the startle index. You hit 'em and they're dead in one swat. They don't shit on your pillow, or rummage through your cabinets, and they don't have big floppy antennae to wave at you. Foremost among the delights of mosquitoes is that they don't seek revenge like earwigs, roaches, and centipedes.

Ants. We all know they're clever and swift—so clever that somehow overnight they managed to build an entire colony under the floor mat on the driver's side of Boner who was parked in the grass, which was now long enough that it was touching the underside of the car, serving as an ant ladder. So I'm driving along and notice that the two ants on the dashboard have become ten. Hmmm. Another minute goes by and I'm cruising along the beautiful blue ocean on the Red Road. It's a sunny day—the wind is blowing through my hair, la la la. I'm having one of those blissed-out in paradise drives singing the Beatles' *Long and Winding Road* because I am driving, you guessed it, a long and winding road. I glance at the dashboard and the ten ants have become fifty. Terror alert is raised to orange. Then I feel a little tickle on my ankle. I look down and there are *thousands* of ants swarming around my feet. Code RED!

Suddenly I am Tippi Hedren in *The Birds* when she finally figures out that the birds in such numbers are actually evil and there has been a quiet conspiracy brewing for some time. I see myself in the black and white film, running down the road, my hair tied into a nice little bun with my arms flailing wildly. I'm looking back while millions of ants are chasing me and biting at my feet and all set to a haunting and thick orchestral soundtrack by Bernard Herrmann. It's Hitchcock's new movie, *The Ants,* and I'm the hapless star about to be eaten alive.

Don't panic, I told myself. Slow the car down. No acci-
dents—better to be bitten into anaphylactic shock than to die from
a car accident. Don't skid off the road. I pull over and throw the
door open, jump out into the middle of the road without looking—fortunately there were no other cars—and scream into the
jungle, "Why meeeeee!? Leave me aloooooone!" I stamped my feet
in a temper tantrum to get the ants off my legs. I yanked the floor
mat out, swatted the ones that got on my hand just from doing that
and then surveyed the car.

Ants were swarming all over the transmission, the seat, the steering wheel, the dashboard, the windshield, and mirror. And they
were all toting their precious little eggs. They were mobilized—time
to get out of Dodge, quite literally. "Oh god," I thought, "What in
the *hell* am I going to do?" I could just imagine the forest spirits of
native Hawaiians tittering at me from behind the ohia trees.

I calmed myself down and realized I was screwed—plain and
simple; they had won. I was too far from home to abandon the car
and walk anywhere. There was no way to get a colony of ants out of
the car without spraying them with poison. I could make a little
bridge and invite each one to come and walk the plank off the car
like a reverse Noah's ark. No way. I was in an environmental ethical
crisis right there on the roadside.

What I needed was a spray bottle of poison and the only thing
between me and a handy little can of mass ant death was a five
minute drive home with the ants swarming over my body—five
minutes surrendered to bug world. I thought it through: For five
minutes, I'm going to just sit down in that ant colony and be an ant.
Yep, I have to do it. What else am I going to do?

OK, so I'm going to do it. I've decided. Yep. OK, but when? I
could wait a while and then miss my inspection appointment in
town. Just do it. The longer you wait, the harder it's going to be.
Just do it, you goddamn little sissy. Get in the car. Just *get in the car!*

You know that feeling when you have a BandAid stuck on your hairy arm because the man-hating nurse at the clinic where you just gave blood figures she can extract some reparations out of you because you're male? She slaps a big sticky BandAid on your hairy gorilla arm knowing it's going to hurt like hell for you to yank it off. And so you sit there thinking, I guess I could wait until the glue on this eventually gives out, maybe slip some Goo Gone under there and slide it off. Or I could cut all my arm hair off under the bandage with an X-acto knife and leave a big rectangular bald spot on my arm like a crop circle in a field that would take six months to grow back. Or I could just be a man and yank the bandage off and scream like a little girl. You shudder at the limitations of your gender-role conditioning and you give the bandage the big yank and you suffer in silence. Big boys don't cry, after all. And so it was that I faced the dilemma of the five-minute ant drive.

I took a deep breath and jumped aboard the anthill on wheels. I figured that if I wiggled and slapped every part of my body every two seconds, no ant would have time to bite me. And so I did this little patty-cake dance on my whole body all the way back home.

I drove with my big toe on the gas pedal avoiding contact with anything. I kept my left leg suspended in the air and held the wheel with my fingertips in between slap-fests. From the side of the road I'm sure I looked like some nutcase just out of the asylum on a day pass, which, here in Puna, is not really an unusual sight.

Squealing around the corner past the yogis weeding the garden at the retreat center, I gained sight of the house and put the car into neutral, threw the door open, engaged the parking brake and jumped out of the car. Boner came to a stop on his own with me standing by, swatting the remaining dozen or so ants on my legs.

The rest is just a sad story for the ants. They were wasted in a terrible holocaust of pine-scented dioxins. And for the rest of the day I had to pick the remains of them out of crevices and off the seats with a few bedraggled ones stumbling out, doing their death spiral and landing on me as I continued my errands. I was perfectly happy to face an eventual brain tumor to be rid of the ants. Oddly I didn't sustain a single bite from this joy ride with the ants. I think they may not have been the biting kind. Ooopsie.

Now, that should have been enough close encounters with arthropods for any one human being. I felt that I had endured my bug allotment for the day, but no. After my beautiful nightly starlit swim at Kalani, I was sitting in the hot tub noticing that the Big Dipper was so far to the north and that the Milky Way was so bright that one can practically read the *New York Times* by it (if only I could find a *New York Times*). I was leaning back and relaxing in the tub when a giant cockroach jumped onto my back like some bandit in the Wild West would jump onto a train from an overpass.

Well, I gave the roach one hell of a ride—I flipped out so wildly that I banged my arm on the side of the tub, bruising myself. The 4-inch little bundle of hell landed on the side of the tub and just stood there facing me down—kind of like Cheech and Chong would have cast a look of indignance: "Sheet man, is dat all da ride I get?"

What could I do? I was naked—no bottle of spray handy, no deadly flip flop for you, you little bastard. All I had to do was create the tsunami of its life and so I washed the little brown bugger over the gunwale to the ground. Time to get outta here before it scales the side of the tub in a heated rush of revenge.

I showered and dried off, now completely paranoid. I watched my every step for moving things. I got to the car and I opened the door to find another lovely 4-inch friend coyly batting its big antennae at me from my seat as if to say, "Hi honey, I've been waiting for you to take me home. Shall we go now?"

This time I deployed my killer flip-flop! I got in one good swat from the dreaded Old Navy sandal of death. The roach flew into the air, landed on the floor on its back and immediately went into its death rattle, which is a fast and furious run-like-hell response, only they can't run, because they're flipped helplessly onto their backs. Once I had smacked one in the living room at Don's with my sandal and managed to disable its starboard side legs. So it flipped onto its back and was kicking itself in circles like some dolt paddling a canoe from one side only.

After the ants incident, I wised up and kept that bottle of pine-scented insecticide in the car. I pulled it from under the seat and bathed the little fucker in it. Minutes later it was *still* alive with guts hanging out and its skin burning from this napalm in a bottle.

Do you see how dastardly I'm becoming? No more Mr. Let's Take the Spider Gently Outside in a Little Square of Toilet Paper and Release Him. No way, man. If it's a bug and it's in the house or the car, I'm pounding it all the way to purgatory. Even if it's not in the house, if it's just thinking of coming in the house, it's dead. Bud's words of wisdom on murder once again had incredible relevance to life in the jungle.

And so here I am at half past midnight at Don's house, unable to calm down and relax for fear that all I need to complete a perfect day in bug hell is to have a poisonous centipede crawl into bed and sting me. I'm still getting over a nasty case of bed bugs that drilled into my left foot leaving a Cassiopeia-like trail of bite marks. Incidentally, I decided to squeeze one of the fluid-filled blisters out yesterday and it squirted a big load right into my face. Nice. I was sure a bed bug would come to life, born of the splat on my face like a scene out of *Alien.*

Now, any little noise in the house and I think some roach's uncle has come to avenge their family's tragedy. I'm certain there's a syndicate—a Mafia-like network of insects that takes care of its own. If a loose thread from my shorts grazes my leg hairs I automatically go into a slapping frenzy like Scarlett O'Hara slapping Prissy. If I see some dark spot on the floor, I launch into a tap dancing routine like

I was in *Stomp*. I inspect everything carefully before I put it on, open it up, or sit on it. I think Xanax is in store for this evening: I'm out of happy places to go to and I have a house to build.

Love, Seaweed

PS—I saw a very cool gadget at a friend's house: a battery operated tennis racket with electrified metal mesh that zaps bugs when you wave it over them. Their little carcasses fry with an audible sizzle. Oh god, what will become of me?

9

August 13, 2005

THE WALLS GO UP

Day Sixty-Nine

Before a brilliant person begins something great,
they must look foolish in the crowd.
—From the *I Ching*

Last week I was heading down to the beach for another day of waiting for construction to begin when a large flatbed truck went rushing by with a delivery of lumber. I saw a blur of "Happy Gilmore" spray-painted in big red letters on the side. I turned right back around, scampered up the guava trail trying not to twist an ankle, rushed to my car and raced to the lot to make sure they were delivering my first load of lumber to the correct location.

A large, friendly Hawaiian driver got out and introduced himself as Psalms. The Christian missionaries have certainly imprinted themselves on the culture if Hawaiian families are naming their kids after books in the *Old Testament*. While his truck idled, we talked for quite a while about his family, the Hawaiian language, and public schools. He told me that Hawaiian is taught in the public schools until 4th grade at which point students are educated in English.

Psalms returned to the cab and backed the truck up the side of the lot, unhitched the lumber from the bed, revved the engine insanely high and then engaged the clutch. In what seemed a really crude manner of delivery, my lumber was literally dumped on the property with only a minor amount of damage to the wood. The truck left big gouges in the cinders where the tires spun out.

This lumber dump contained ground floor building materials including 2x4s for the walls, 4x4s for the lanai posts, 2x10s for the joists, plywood for shear walls, nails and all the hardware needed. There would be a siding delivery, a second floor delivery, roof trusses, and so on. I looked forward to more chats with Psalms.

With permits stamped and supplies delivered, we were ready to begin the framing, truly the most exciting part of the building. Scott and Rowdie, the framers, finally started on Thursday. They pulled up in an old Ford pickup with rusting roof rack and out popped the two builders on their last year or so of being considered handsome. Too many years in the sun and bad food had their bodies looking a little worn out. They each had cigarettes and coffee in their hands. Nearly everyone in construction smokes, has a dog or two, and brings their own stereo system to blast rock and roll. I guess I couldn't expect to hear Brahms piano quartets or Rufus Wainwright in a smoke-free work environment. I got my earplugs ready.

True to form, Scott pulled out his beat up boom box, plugged it in and searched for one of only two radio stations available out here. They landed on the one that played classic rock—Beatles, Pink Floyd, and the Rolling Stones—without any objection from me. Out also jumps a crippled dog, Honey, who is a cream-colored, mellow pit bull who sat tied to the support poles of the construction tent watching the goings-on.

I sat cross-legged with Scott and Rowdie in the middle of the slab as we unrolled the blueprints like we were unrolling a treasure map. I in my naïveté made some sort of dumb speech that they were building my *home,* not just a house … that I would be living in this house and maybe would die in this house and that I wanted it to be built with care and respect. I went on and on while their eyes glazed over.

I stood up now and paced while I yammered and gesticulated. "We will be working together for the next six months and I want this to be a positive experience for everyone. I don't want to hear any offensive remarks about gay people, women, or really *anyone.* "

They looked at me strangely as if I had just farted. Imagine that—some guy telling his builders they couldn't be foul-mouthed!

I continued. "I'm here for you guys. If you need anything, just let me know. I value communication and honesty more than anything. If there's something you don't know, just let me know and we'll figure it out."

Before I was finished with my long-winded sermon, they were up and measuring. I stood there with my speech trailing off to a mumble like Don Quixote. They began un-banding and laying the lumber out by size and making lists. They weighted the blueprints down on the slab with lumber, and began making measurements for the first wall.

Scott is the foreman—the brains. Rowdie is the grunt man—as he himself told me. Both are a little surly—they are straight construction workers after all, but easy enough to work with so long as you didn't get in the way and didn't sneak in a little volume reduction on the boom box when they weren't looking. I covered up looking like a fool for my failed motivational speech by making videos and snapping pictures, frequently returning to the car canopy to check my materials lists as if I knew what I was doing. I didn't, but I was learning. Probably the most important things I learned on the first day were: anticipate their needs, keep inventory on the materials and don't *ever* touch the volume on the boom box.

Scott can be a little bossy at times and tends to overuse the word "friggin." I don't think this had anything to do with my request for decency—I think it's more that his daughter Amber often accompanies him to jobs. And so an edict from Scott goes something like this, "Hey, uh David," he would say with a lit cigarette bobbing up and down on his lips with every word, "See that friggin board over there? Friggin HPM delivered you the wrong friggin size. Call them and talk to the friggin contractor's desk and tell them you want a friggin refund." At one point I said to him, "Man that's a lot of friggins." I laughed. He didn't.

Rowdie snapped a line on the slab with chalk and began cutting lumber into pieces and laying them out while Scott measured and marked the next cuts. I made a video of the first cut that broke the silence of the meadow. My neighbors slammed their windows shut—they knew the score—that sound was the beginning of a colossal amount of noise, dust, paint, smoke, and fumes headed their way for the next year. I felt bad for them. Scott and Rowdie continued cutting and nailing the first wall together horizontally on the slab.

I spent the hours of the first day kicking around the lot, fiddling with lumber and nails. Within in a couple hours, the western wall was ready to lift into place. It was placed at the edge of the slab with a piece of tarpaper underneath it and they grunted, shook, and strained to lift it into place while I made a video. I had to stop to help, as they simply couldn't get it more than 45 degrees off the slab. The three of us got it perpendicular to the slab and Scott braced it with boards. Rowdie held it firmly and Scott tapped it with the nailgun—*phit-phit*. A first wall was up! I walked around and around trying to imagine what life would be like inside the house based on one wall. By the end of the day we had two walls and I was ready to start playing house. Monday they promised we'd have the remaining two walls. The following week they expected they'd start the second floor.

Vienna, Paris, Puna

I was deliriously happy to see the house taking shape and spent the weekend celebrating with some new friends. Any time I'm new in a place it takes me a while to understand the social scene—especially for someone who would rather hold on to an ideal than face reality. Or perhaps it's that I'm basically clueless about the vibe of a place when I'm distracted by the newness of it.

And then the revelation hit me like a speeding Ford Taurus wagon with the bumper hanging off: there are extremely few people with any refinement here in eastern Hawaii. With a few exceptions, the new locals of lower Puna are largely hucksters, mountain folk, jungle boys, white trash, new age seekers, bliss ninnies, stoners, sex addicts, or the mentally-ill. I only know of one man who keeps a real job—a mailman.

This really is the new Wild Wild West. What California was to the gold prospectors in 1849, Hawaii is to the homesteaders of Puna. People flock here to get rich on real estate speculation, or simply to drop out. They are not the educated who move here to work on their postdoc dissertations in the quiet nights of the jungle. Like the settlers across the prairies of 19th century America, the folks here come with a pioneering sense of adventure. They come to build their zero lot line homes, stake a claim, and screw their brains out in their middle-age years. They don't pack their degrees, art collections, and crates of literature. The effete stay back in "the States" as they did 200 years ago in the northeast. (I am consciously calling the mainland the States.)

Like the Okies toting only their Bibles when they headed west from the dust bowl, settlers in Hawaii today come with books like

The Celestine Prophecy and *The Da Vinci Code*—fiction taken as non-fiction. They come with DVDs like Suze Orman's *The Courage to Be Rich* and *What the Bleep Do We Know?,* favoring platitudes, feel good solutions, and personal transformations. Wisdom and knowledge here are gained intuitively or by hearsay. If one is ever in doubt of this, pick up any hitchhiker along Puna's Red Road, and ask for some medical advice or try to have a political discussion. You'll hear everything from the likes of fermented noni juice being a cure-all, to 9/11 being a conspiracy, to letting flies eat the dead flesh out of your staph infection—nothing about a good shot in the ass with penicillin.

As you may have guessed, I can sometimes be a little blinded by beauty. Sometimes it takes me a little too long to get the real vibe of a person or a place. I shall now outline for you how I came to realize that Puna is not Paris:

First Clue

Recently I attended a party at a rather up-market home that was recently featured in the *New York Times.* I imagined that we would be feasting on fresh fruit drinks with Grey Goose vodka and caram-bola slices placed on the edge of each glass. I expected to be greeted with a tray of herbed bruschetta with goat cheese and smoked salmon mousse with capers. Instead, I was greeted at the door with a tray of Pigs in a Blanket and Miller Lite in the can. I felt like I had arrived in Dix Hills, Long Island, a subdivision known for pricey suburban real estate and its gaudy inhabitants who built their empires in the blue collar trades, drove Lincoln town cars and wore rabbit fur coats with fringy boots.

Second Clue

Remember Bud, the guy with the bad tan who said, "When you live in the jungle, you learn how to murder"? I saw him limping along by the roadside a couple days ago, dirty, stinky, and tired. Bud had just spent the whole day mowing the lawn at Kalani, bouncing on the hard tractor seat. His rump was a little tender as if he had been paddled at an English boarding school. I offered him a ride home, which meant discretely rolling down all the windows before stopping, if you know what I mean. I jammed all four fingers on the down buttons and applied the brakes.

Bud lives in the jungle with innumerable cats and admittedly questionable hygiene. Giving him a ride to work is better than a ride home. When I pulled up to the two palm trees that flanked his driveway to drop him off, he fumbled with the door. He simply couldn't figure out the handle and lock. I clicked the electric lock release and pointed to the handle, instructing him to pull on it and then push the door open.

"I'm not used to getting in and out of cars with doors," he groused. He was referring to the quintessential "Puna ride:" an old car with no doors, no muffler, and no hubcaps.

He was met by his sexy young boyfriend who came out of the shack with his shorts barely clinging to his slender hips, with Velcro fly already open, Bud, who is 62, coughed up a gravelly laugh and disappeared down his driveway with his lover on his arm. This is a gay version of the *Dukes of Hazard* and the young boyfriend was Daisy Duke—barefoot and trying to get pregnant.

Third Clue

Two nights ago I had dinner in Pahoa with a couple formerly from the Central Valley of California, the only noteworthy virtue of which is its proximity to San Francisco. These guys left the Valley with Kate Wolf singing in their ears, "… there's no gold in California, and the hills turn brown in the summertime." They too, staked their claim at the 19th parallel buying several lots of land here. Over the worst Chinese dinner I have ever eaten, I asked these men if they ever went to San Francisco when they lived so close for 20 years. They both shook their heads. "Oh, well, once or twice. We didn't really care for it." I sat in shock, unable to speak.

As I pushed slimy, gray bits of what I think was chicken (maybe it was peacock) around a plastic plate, I mentioned that one could find fantastic, fresh Chinese food in San Francisco, unlike the mystery meat clinging to my fork. My point was lost.

"You mean you never ate at House of Nanking or Tommy Toy's in San Francisco?" I asked.

"No, the parking in San Francisco is terrible. Couldn't fit the truck in those teeny spaces. Now quit complaining and eat yer chicken parts. We gotta get some meat on yer bones—you're so skeeeny." I was told.

Noticing that I didn't eat much of this pathetic meal was inspiration for a sermon from one of the mountain men about the need to fatten me up. No doubt this was a throwback to the infamous Donner Party crossing of the Sierra-Nevadas in a winter snowstorm and the cannibalism that ensued. To these mountain men, a bespectacled guy skipping around Puna in red "fruit boots" with a 135-pound frame looked like a fine appetizer on a cold night, of which here in the tropics, I might point out, we have none.

I've also come to realize that as a relative latecomer to the scene, I have taken on the role of a modern-day, gay version of Father Damien known for his Christian crusade of propriety telling the Hawaiians to put some clothes on. Damien came by ship from Belgium in the mid-19th century to shape up the heathen masses of Hawaii who were still reeling from the destruction of their "savage" kapu mythology and customs. He is remembered for taking care of the lepers on Molokai, but also for introducing thorny ground cover in Puna, ushering in a painful end to the Hawaiians' halcyon barefoot days.

My thoughts heralding the virtues of western medicine, the *New York Times,* and classical music are completely denounced by the new Hawaiians who are contented drinking a little fermented noni juice, telling a tall tale, and listening to *Kenny G.*

Monday, as I stood on my slab conducting the framers (in my own Quixotic way), a pony-tailed neighbor stopped by to tell me that President Bush was being impeached. I was, of course, doubtful of this news.

"Some half-baked fringe notion or is this legit?" I asked.

"No, this it. This is the real thing, man," the former Californian replied.

A wicked little smile turned up the corners of my mouth imagining the arrogant president being overturned as the tide of public opinion shifted. I couldn't wait to grab my laptop and head down to the Kalani café to read the news. When I got there, I looked on the websites of the *New York Times,* NPR, CNN, and *Democracy Now*—nothing about an impeachment. Uh huh. I felt so stupid.

Sister Damien just became more resolute than ever. Maybe it's time to start a Sunday school. We'll start with grooming techniques, move on to fashionable footwear and eyewear selection, and end up with a lecture on legitimate news sources.

With love from the jungle,

Sister Damien

10

August 18, 2005

WALMART AND DA JESUS BOOK IN THE NEW HAWAII

Day Seventy-Four

I heard it myself: "Mahalo for kokua with your keiki." That's what the voice said over the Walmart public address system. Subject, object, and predicate in Hawaiian, prepositions in English.

What, you might ask, was I doing in Wal-Mart? Someone with my values never shops in Wal-Mart. I confess that I compromised my mainland virtues and have shopped at the dreaded Wal-Mart. If you've been reading these journal entries regularly, you know that moving to Hawaii has led me to compromise many of my beliefs, from buying a new car to using pesticides, to rampant jungle massacres of helpless frogs. I have not, however, done the little dance of allegiance to Sam Walton that employees perform during their meetings like good little capitalist pawns.

I apologize for my transgression—it's just that Hilo has limited shopping options and Wal-Mart has a few things that no one else has. (Yes, I know, it's *because* of Wal-Mart that there are no other options. But what can I do when I have to fulfill my suburban jungle needs? On the mainland you have choices. In Hawaii you have Wal-Mart with its large Spam section.)

Anyway, there I was in Wal-Mart, navigating my skinny self through the obstacle course of the morbidly obese in a pre- and post-diabetic wonderland of junk. I dart through the narrow aisles of plastic and blinky things with my hand-held basket, of which the store has about three because no one who waddles through the sliding glass doors of Wal-Mart, heading for the shrine of Chinese-manufactured crap, buys just a *few* things. People go for the jumbo size everything, heaped up on carts bigger than my car.

Who among you has not at least walked with horror through the highly-waxed aisles of Wal-Mart to witness the hoarding of cheap goods, perhaps even to shamefully sneak a few into your own cart? Most people with any righteous values regret the one or two times that they've shopped at Wal-Mart—like the time when you needed that knife to eat the pineapple still warm from the field—where else do you go? Then you know what I mean. Wal-Mart is an American phenomenon that has imposed itself globally. And here it is in a place that is questionably American: Hawaii. In fact, the Hawaii stores are the most successful stores in the chain. It is a snake in the grass plunked down at the center of an asphalt heat island in view of Mauna Kea, the tallest island volcano in the world.

For those of you not familiar with the Hawaiian sovereignty movement, the few descendents of native stock here have launched a campaign to take back the Kingdom of Hawaii. The Hawaiian flag is flown upside down in distress. More than just an inverted flag, it is a movement to empower Hawaii as a sovereign nation and seeks redress from the United States for its illegal military occupation and dissolution of the Hawaiian monarchy.

It's a sensitive issue for all who reside in Hawaii. We can no longer deny the wrongdoing of the United States: In 1993, the United States Congress passed, and President Bill Clinton signed Public Law 103–150 that officially apologizes for the overthrow of the Kingdom of Hawaii. But the overthrow happened in 1893 when William McKinley was president. Since then, much American water has flowed under the bridge, and sadly, the vestiges of old Hawaii are almost completely gone. Although I think that supporting the Hawaiian sovereignty movement is the *right* thing to do—mostly for preservation of the ecology, the land, the traditions, and the language, it is terribly unlikely that the genie will ever go back in the bottle.

I am curious what a sovereign Hawaii would look like, should that ever occur. Would it include the likes of Wal-Mart, Spam, and ATVs—just a few destructive American imports that Hawaiians seem to enjoy? The sovereignty movement, like the Akaka Bill before congress that would provide Native Hawaiians with federal recognition much like Native Americans have, will likely result in nothing more than a gesture to the once island nation. Like them or not, Wal-Mart and Starbucks, mosquitoes, and the coqui frogs are here to stay.

Wal-Mart, however, does its part to contribute its tacit support of the Hawaiian culture (or is it to placate their Hawaiian employees?) by making announcements on the PA system in "Hanglish"—what I'm calling the fusion of Hawaiian and English, not to be confused with pidgin. Hanglish is when you go to a party and someone comes around with a tray of appetizers and says, "Pupus any one?" I have found myself irreverently giggling at the use of that word.

You'll also hear the fusion at the farmer's market when the karaoke singer makes an announcement that the food she just ate from booth 13 is, "ono-licious." This is actually a Hanglish redundancy—"ono" means *delicious.* You might find yourself buying a "huli" chicken *(rotisserie)* or you'll see it on signs that say, "Kapu! Keep Out." (Kapu is one of the most important Hawaiian words meaning *forbidden.*)

All the street names are now in Hawaiian, which means having to chew through many consonants and what always seems like an extra syllable or two. The Hawaiian language, which was never written before the Europeans arrived and assisted them in transliteration, uses only eight consonants as opposed to English's 21. For example, the coastal road in Puna is Kalapana-Kopoho and the main street in Hilo is Kanoelehua, or as Patrick calls it "canoli hula." The last Queen of Hawaii's name was Lili'uokalani, shortened to "Lil" for those who get tripped up on the seven syllables required to say her name in full.

English really isn't any more sensible or easy, with words like indubitable, dysmorphophobia, electroencephalograph, and anything ending with "ough." And how many definitions of the word "run" are there in English? My American Heritage lists 34 verb and 33 noun uses. We also have odd quirks like "valuable" and "invaluable," the "in-" added to the front makes valuable even more so. And sanction means both approval and a penalty. So I don't want to hear anyone making fun of Hawaiian being an odd language with words meaning too many different things. It's just a matter of familiarity.

Isabella Bird wrote in her travelogue of the "Sandwich Islands" (as Hawaii was known in 1875), that the Hawaiian language sounds, "… more like water rippling than human speech." She was known for being a little culturally insensitive, but in *this* case she's right—hearing the language without any knowledge of meaning, it does sound a bit like water lapping up on rocks. What does an English word like "gynecological" sound like to those who don't understand—a turkey gobbling?

I've yet to hear Hawaiian spoken in any casual setting. In its purest form, it is mostly only spoken fluently by scholars any more, and many of them, ironically are haoles. Wresting the bastardized Hawaiian language from the likes of that woman on the horn at Wal-Mart is perhaps another reason to keep those willowy white folk around.

> *Pidgin: a simplified language made up of elements of two or more languages used as a communication tool between speakers whose native languages are different.*

Pidgin on the other hand, is a low-prestige, reductionist language wrought to imperfection by the generations of Filipino, Chinese, and Japanese immigrants who were imported to work the pineapple and sugar cane fields over the last century and a half. I first encountered pidgin when I met a man at the Steam Vents in Pahoa.

The Vents is a remnant of an old lava flow that left small caves which fill with steam as rainwater enters still cooling fissures. The Vents sit in the middle of a field of wild orchids at the intersection of natives, tourists, hippies, and gays who come to steam themselves, relax, and cruise for sex. You can guess which of these reasons brought me to the Vents.

The afternoon of my first encounter with pidgin, I met a straight guy in the main cave who spoke with a heavy accent that I couldn't quite place. I guessed from his face that he was Filipino-Hawaiian. That was correct. I asked him what his accent was assuming Tagalog was his first language.

"I speak pidgin," he said.

"What *is* pidgin, really?" I asked.

"Broken English."

"Broken English is a language?" I queried with raised eyebrow doubting a language that sounded something like English but bears such a heavy accent that I could barely understand him. He doesn't speak Tagalog or Hawaiian so I wondered where the heavy accent was coming from.

"Yeah, braddah. Broken English pidgin!" he emphatically replied.

Pidgin, like this man, is a language of few words. We resorted to kissing. I guess he wasn't *that* straight.

Pidgin in recent times has become elevated to a written language. By this virtue, broken English has indeed become a language—and really, it is the primary living language of Hawaii. At first I found myself snottily thinking one cannot have a language that is in itself a reduction of a language and call it legitimate, even publish books in pidgin. But then I learned that the people who came to Hawaii in the last 150 years joined a melting pot of machete-wielding workers bent over in the fields of sugar cane and pineapple. Of course everyone came with their own language and a little broken English too, with which to negotiate with the lords of fructose. But when you've got Hawaiians, Japanese, Filipino, and Chinese folks working together, the common language became this broken English. This is the pidgin of Hawaii today. You hear it on the radio, at the checkout counters at the grocery store in Pahoa, and among the tradesmen of my house construction.

What I found particularly fascinating was when I spoke to the plumbers about the job—their foreman spoke perfect English to me regarding costs and timeline. But when he spoke to his co-workers about work actualities, he switched into pidgin with its singsong prosody. His English jumbled with pidgin words and a strong accent, made it impossible for me to understand what he was saying.

Pidgin has become so legitimized in Hawaii that there is now a pidgin dictionary and even a pidgin Bible. Following is a passage from *Da Jesus Book, the Hawaiian Pidgin New Testament* published by the Wycliffe Bible Translators. Copyright, 2000. This is not a joke, folks. Dis fo real …

Page iii

"Dis book tell bout Jesus and his ancesta guys. He da Christ, da Spesho Guy God Wen Send. He from King David ohana, an David, he from Abraham ohana. Dis Jesus ohana. Get fourteen faddas from Abraham to David: Abraham, he Isaac fadda. Isaac, he Jacob fadda. Jacob, he Judah faddah, and all Judah bruddas, he dea fadda too …

Jesus wen start fo show da guys he teaching how he gotta go Jerusalem an suffa plenny ova dea. All da older leada guys, dey da one dat goin make Jesus suffa, an dey da ones dat goin kill him. But he say he goin come back alive day numba tree afta dey kill um."

If you read it fast, it sounds like Brer Rabbit has been thrown into a pineapple patch. By the way, "ohana" is the one Hawaiian word used, meaning *family*.

Welcome to da new Hawaii. It is part Hawaiian, part Asian, part haole. Part Wal-Mart, part English, part pidgin. So if you stop by the old wood-framed Opihikao Church on Kalapana-Kapoho Road tucked in among the old growth mangoes and coconut trees in coastal Puna, you will hear the murmurs of pidgin. You will see Spam dishes served at the Sunday potluck. You will see round brown faces and angular white faces. You will see aloha shirts, muu'muus, and slippahs. You will hear a Christian sermon spoken in English with hymns sung in Hawaiian accompanied by the ukulele band. And, by the way, lest you make a haole fool of yourself, that's pronounced oooh-ku-lay-lay, not you-ku-lay-lee.

Love, Seaweed

11

August 21, 2005

THE MILK MOUSTACHE DISASTER

Day Seventy-Seven

The crew and I have been working diligently at the construction site framing up the first floor and reaching up toward the second. The second-floor supplies arrived with Psalms doing another pop-the-clutch routine at the side of the lot, which is steadily filling up with construction debris. I shuddered thinking about all the trees that came down in the mainland northwest for this house. At least I didn't order decking, siding, and flooring made of wood.

Scott and Rowdie go about their work dutifully, ducking under the construction tent when the rains cycle through. And then five minutes later, they're back out working in the sun, smoking cigarettes and singing out of tune to the boom box. The rain comes in waves across the lava flow from the northeast born on the trade winds: a few minutes of rain every 20 minutes.

Not too much of my presence is required on-site at the moment. Scott is clearly a very competent builder and bosses us all around with his unassailable authority—he's never wrong about *anything*. When I'm not on site, I make trips to Hilo to order supplies and pick out cabinetry, flooring, and make endless aesthetic decisions. Later on, I work the phone for at least a couple hours each day at Don's jungalow herding contractors, suppliers, and dealing with the banks. At the moment it all seems to be going smoothly—I anticipate what the contractors need next, and do whatever it takes to get it to the site.

Yesterday, I got my first glimpse of the ocean view standing atop the ladder poking up through the floor joists of the second floor on the house. It was terribly exciting to see over the treetops to the blue in the distance. It is a personal triumph for me to be able to afford this much debt and this much view. I stood there spellbound until Scott told me to get off the ladder.

Before the weekend, Scott gave me the assignment to get the primer coat of paint on the trim and the fascia before the roof went on. He suggested renting a sprayer and so I did. I now concede that this would fall into the category of "Don't Ever Do *That* Again!" I spent many hours and three trips to Home Depot picking out paint colors and testing them on boards at the site. I took a photograph of the house and produced a mockup of various color schemes in Photoshop on my laptop and showed them around to friends for opinions. I decided on celery for the siding and red wine for the trim. Choosing colors was basically the end of the fun part of painting, and also where my competency ran out. I loaded the monstrously heavy buckets of primer and paint into the car. The buckets were so heavy that I had to waddle with them between my legs when I was unloading them at Don's house.

What was needed for a good application of paint was an airless sprayer and a calm day. And so it was when dawn came and I raced up the hill to be the first one at Pahoa Hardware to get the sprayer. I returned to the job site and loaded up the sprayer with the primer. I had already tarped the window and door cutouts of the downstairs so that I would not get any paint on the concrete slab—the surface needed to be kept clean if it was to be etched, stained, and waxed to glossy perfection as planned.

The sprayer sucked up the primer and at about the same time that I pressed the trigger on the spray hose, I felt the first tickle of breeze on my arm hairs. The land was beginning to warm up and the breezes were starting. Well, once I get started on something, there's virtually no stopping me. If a gale force wind came, I'd be upwind trying to get the angle of the sprayer just right working with the wind so that it carried paint to the house.

And that is almost precisely what happened. In the next few hours as I worked through the primer, the winds increased. I stopped briefly to move my car first across the street. Then down the block. I made sure I tarped my neighbor's truck. I could see the wind taking paint hundreds of feet from the house. It was getting out of hand fast. Half of the paint never hit the house. In my state of low blood sugar combined with the adrenaline to get the job done by the end of the day, I tripped on a 5-gallon bucket of primer, spilling the thick white goo all over the lava. I was horrified by the toxicity of this going down into the ground and ultimately into the sea. I only hoped it would dry before it made it to the dolphins and sea turtles. I felt like Joseph Hazelwood, the notorious captain of the Exxon Valdez.

Stopping to try and mop up my first chemical spill, I discovered the *real* horror: the sound of water dripping. After owning three homes, I've learned a couple important details about home construction and ownership: follow the water and follow the noises. I had previously drilled holes in the plywood sub-flooring upstairs to allow collected rainwater (there is still no roof) to drain down to the first floor. I peeked my head inside the tarped downstairs doors and witnessed the tragedy of white puddles of primer collecting on the concrete slab. Great, my precious concrete slab had a giant milk moustache. I had not accounted for the wind taking the airborne primer and dumping it on the upstairs floor, which had water pooling on the floor from the night's rain. The primer then drained through the weep holes with the water to the first floor. *God almighty.*

I watched in disbelief as a dozen white waterfalls of primer trickled all over my precious slab. How could I possibly have planned for what seemed like a conspiracy of events? Humiliated and disheartened by such a minor oversight and such a major gaffe, I continued. Moving on is the most valuable lesson I've picked up about building: don't stop to grieve a mistake—just keep going. Put aside your feelings for the moment (something I find terribly challenging) and find an immediate solution. I knew, though, that one day I would have one hell of a balloon payment of grief for kicking over that bucket of primer, for the primer on the slab, and for all that I could not even imagine would happen in the coming months of construction.

There was no chance of hosing the slab down without a power washer, which was 17 miles away in Pahoa at the nearest hardware store. In the tropical heat with trade winds, it would be dry by that time. It would just be a slab with primer stains on it. I went on to do the trim.

I cleaned out the paint sprayer in buckets of water I filled with a siphon hose out of the catchment tank, and loaded up the trim paint. I opened the first bucket of trim color, stirred it with a stick and put the intake nozzle into the rich, wine-colored paint.

On went the first coat of what looked like Pepto-Bismol trim paint. *Hot pink?* How could that be? The boards on which I painted the trim samples looked fine—a deep red wine color. Another hard-won lesson: first primer whatever wood you use for color tests. I had stupidly tested the paint on un-primered bare wood, which is darker than wood that has been painted with primer. The trim color on un-primered wood looked as it should: like wine. The trim color on primered wood looked like Barbie's vinyl hot pants.

Oh good lord, what have I done? I'm either going to have a pink trimmed house, or I will have to throw out all that paint and switch colors, or I'm going to be doing multiple coats of paint. I imagined everyone laughing at me and just assumed no one would ever want a boyfriend with a pink house. Nix on the first option. My environmental ethics would not allow me to discard that much paint and so I committed to painting the house four times. At twice the cost of paint and time expenditure, I did just that. With each successive coat of pink, I finally achieved the desired red wine color.

Never again the sprayer. Never again the red wine.

Aloha, Seaweed

PS—Next week Bud will explain his latest quote, "When I get paid, I'm getting a toilet and a 22. But it ain't for shootin' pigs."

12

August 28, 2005

LOST PUPPIES

Day Eighty-Four

To live in this world you must be able to do three things:
to love what is mortal;
to hold it against your bones knowing your own life depends on it;
and, when the time comes to let it go, to let it go.
—Mary Oliver

Near the end of August here in Kehena Beach, the guava and mango trees give up their fruit with embarrassing abundance. Anywhere you walk, the acrid rotting smell of tropical fruit laid to waste in piles of seeds and skins mixes with the smell of the ocean and the sweet perfumes of the plumeria trees. Avocados too, smashed in greasy greens and golds litter the roadside, a familiar color palette you'd expect if you were making guacamole, not taking a walk.

While high tech freaks and pyromaniacs are putting the final touches on their Burning Man contraptions in California; while folks are preparing for Labor Day weekend barbecues all across the country, summer gives an almost unnoticed nod toward autumn here on the Big Island. The days are barely shorter; the nights are only a couple degrees cooler. But somehow, the fruit trees get their cue to start dumping fruit.

It was around this time that I had seriously begun to question my desire to live here. It's not much of a secret now that I have found the community a bit disappointing. Or was it that I'm just new and this is typical of a move anywhere? Was it that I just had too high expectations? Or was it that there is not a decent shoe store any-where on this island? All these questions swam circles in my head until I quieted them with a shot of tequila, a hit of Xanax, or some yoga on the beach at sunrise.

All the quieting done, and still another Saturday night had come and gone without any one to hang out with. One rainy night look-ing for a movie in Don's guest room, I pawed through a collection of moldy videotapes looking for a movie. I saw *Raising Arizona* on the top shelf and pulled it down. I watched it with tears in my eyes—sunshine, blue skies, open space, the desert. I was homesick for a place that I left in a huff. Had I made a big mistake?

I began sinking into a detached stupor. I invented lovers on the phone, as the Janis Ian song goes, "… who called to say, come dance with me." I murmured the vague obscenities at forty-one. Couldn't she just revise that song to include a little something about being alone at mid-life on a remote tropical island, building a house that you can't afford and trying desperately to fit in with a crowd that really isn't worth the effort? Oh god, another night of tequila lay ahead. And I'm not even a drinker, really—I'm just trying to medi-cate away the loneliness.

Slipping into an admittedly pathetic poor-me-in-paradise state of mind, I plotted my exit strategy, again. There's really only so much quieting one can do about not fitting in before it just becomes abundantly clear that the royal "we" have plunked ourselves down in the wrong place and it's time to make a change. That we would be me, and that place would be Hawaii. How many times in my life have I run away? This time, I have to stay and finish what I've started. Perhaps I need a more sustainable solution.

Letting go of all expectations was, of course, a possibility often revisited in my life. Yes, let go. OK, I let go and it's still just me and my books, reading, and running to the café with laptop tucked under my arm to upload email, sitting at the ice cream bar at Kalani watching the pretty people prancing around in various states of sexual ambiguity, androgyny, and upper middle-class white angst.

How many times can I meet the same person who does not recall meeting me before I swat them with a rotten papaya (at least it would be good for their skin) and tell them to quit smoking pot. It's not even pakalolo anymore. It's dope, dude. And you're smoking too much of it and you've fried your brain, you loser … and *that* is why you don't remember meeting me. Or is it because you don't want to sleep with me because I'm not pretty enough? "Love was meant for beauty queens." Shut up, Janis.

I have to get off this island, I thought. This much paradise is going to kill me. This must be the dreaded *island fever*. Certainly I had heard about it, but somehow I imagined it would be different—that it was a catchy term for claustrophobia, which on an island as big as Hawaii, was not really a problem. I didn't imagine island fever would be about being lonely.

So I treated myself to some lousy goddamn pizza at the Christian pizza parlor in Pahoa. At least if you're going to have scripture on the wall, your pizza better be good or no one will take you seriously—hey, the Shakers learned to make priceless furniture.

Pahoa is the town that deploys security guards at the two grocery stores because the people are so poorly behaved and tweaking on crystal meth, that an after dark visit really seems like you've stepped through the looking glass and entered *Apocalypse Now, Baghdad*

Café and *Friday the Thirteenth* all in one little Wild-West Hawaiian sugar-shack town.

It's a charming town only if you're there in the five minutes of sun it gets each week or you're deluding yourself on some stranger-in-paradise trip and you're just going to experience everything with an open mind. To me, on this night, in this place, I was seeing the undeniable scrappy reality of Pahoa. Everything about it sucked. The pizza sucked. How can they make pizza both dry *and* greasy? Then there's the rain, the deafening coqui frogs, the unlit streets rife with riffraff all conspiring to turn me against this wicked little town.

I comforted myself by knowing that when the house is finished, I'll be out of here and back to Tucson—floating out on the same dream bubble I floated in on. There's no place like the dusty, parched desert with its unassuming middle class, especially when you've spent your summer tortured in the jungles of Hawaii with the painfully poor and the poisoned privileged.

On the way home from my belly-busting pizza, I was singing myself silly in the car listening to my Rufus Wainwright albums, yet again. Rufus has become somewhat of a saving grace to me—his haunting songs and his sweet taffy voice soften all the sharp edges. Somehow I feel that Rufus and I share the same pain, and even though I don't know him personally, it's as if he understands my darkness, that he hears the minor-key chord progressions in my head … and then all of a sudden I hit the brakes and the car screeched and I swerved trying to avoid running over a black dog in the middle of the dark road.

I rolled down my window and yelled at the dog: "Damn dog, get outta the road! Stupid dog. You nearly killed us both." I wished I could have said that to some stinky Scandifarian trust baby strumming his beater guitar and hitchhiking instead of some poor lost dog. It was a little transference going on right there on the Red Road. Mommy needed a Xanax bad. I confess that I felt a little bad yelling at the dog. He was kinda cute, too, though a little desperate with his tongue hanging out and dragging his paws down the middle of the coast road. Desperation and wandering a little lost—we had something in common already.

I continued home and downed a couple shots of Tequila foregoing the Xanax lest I should end up in Betty Ford at the end of the house construction. It was raining again. Fruit flies clung to my book, each one too slow to survive the turning of pages. I finally put myself out of my misery and fell asleep.

The cardinals and the Asian doves start each day here in the jungle. On this new morning, *today,* I am going to get out of bed and do something different. I have to. How about yoga? There must be something to all this stuff about yoga. I'll just get up and try it. I hurl myself out of bed and stumble into my underwear and flip-flops (in pidgin they call them "slippahs") and bolt down the guava trail that runs to the beach.

I stumble down the jagged cliff still wiping the sleep out of my eyes. The sun is just behind the clouds on the horizon. Sunrise is brief here in the tropics, so you have to be at the beach and ready for that two minutes of morning orange or you miss it. Today it was only a silver streak. No color.

I run half way down the black sand beach, shuck my boxers and run into the warm ocean and dodge waves for a few minutes. I'm the only one at the beach. Good, no one will see my bad yoga form. Better yet, I won't have to see anyone who annoys me. I did a few downward-dogs, a few warrior poses and added in some lunges to keep my butt from failing the "pencil test." (To perform the pencil test on yourself, place a pencil beneath the buttocks at the top of your thigh. If the pencil is held in place with your ass sagging over it you have failed the test.)

In a few quick yoga moves I was beginning to see what it was that all these people talk about: the yoga produced a feeling of euphoria while I was standing in a painfully uncomfortable and unnatural position with my limbs shaking. However, my mood was nosing up.

I climbed back up the rocky cliff toward the house to make myself some breakfast. I was about to cross the road when a flash of rickety black fur and clickety toenails on pavement went galloping by. It was the same dog that I had cursed on the road the night before. I imagined that he recognized me and rather than stop and beg for forgiveness for nearly sending me off the road, he passed me by. A wave of guilt overcame me.

Feeling the need to apologize for the night before, I said, "Hey you!" The claptrap of black Lab ground to a stop, once again, right in the middle of the road. His head turned back and his ears went up as if to say, "You talking to me?"

"Yes, you." I squatted down. His tale gave a tentative wag. I noticed that I smiled for the first time in a very long while.

"Come here." I clapped my hands together. He wagged again but didn't come, incredulous that anyone would be calling him over.

"Come here. And get OUT of that road!" I clapped again.

This time he figured I couldn't be talking to anyone else and he lowered his ears and head and approached me limping, with that canine reverence for humans that is so typical of dogs. Maybe this is why we love dogs so much—because they immediately defer to us and offer up humility and cheerfulness without question or judgment. I was in need of a little good cheer and someone to notice me.

He sat down awkwardly on the side of the road, his rear legs just thrown to the side like someone with cerebral palsy might toss their legs aside—he was either injured or handicapped. I wondered if he had fallen out of a truck or if he had been hit. Could it be that he was just exhausted from running scared, or that his paws were worn thin from running on sharp lava? The lava is enough to shred a good pair of shoes in one walk. Imagine how it feels on skin.

I led him back up the guava trail to the house and fed him the only thing I had—some bread at which he sniffed and went for the water instead. I borrowed some dog food from the neighbors Phil and Diane and gave him his first meal while I sat watching with delight.

He cast a look at me when I set down the bowl of food as if to say, "Really? For me?" I put out a folded blanket on which he immediately plunked his crippled body. He slept a lot and seemed really happy to be welcomed to this bipedal pack of animals. I couldn't even get him to leave the porch other than to pee. I left the lanai door open in case he suddenly remembered where he lived—he would be free to go. He seemed so grateful to have a place to call home and didn't want to risk being discarded again. He stayed put.

I posted signs and called the Humane Society. But no one claimed this little gem of an animal with floppy ears and topaz eyes. It was hard for me to comprehend why someone would just throw him away.

A friend took an immediate liking to him and affectionately called him Monkey Pod—after the majestic tropical tree that is everywhere in Hawaii. The name stuck. I repeated it to him hundreds of times with rewards until he made the connection.

Thus began my friendship with the shiny black Labrador with the sad eyes. In just a short time, I have become rather attached to him and his gentle sweetness. He arrived in my life at a crossroads—a time when I needed a friend, someone to care about, who appreciated me and got excited when I came home. I can now see how people become so addicted to pet ownership. You get all the joy of companionship, and other than his coming home covered in dead animal residue once in a while, he's really pretty low maintenance, unlike most people. In a way he doesn't even seem like a dog: he doesn't chew anything or bark. And he seems always so grateful for the smallest things—even just saying his new name or bringing him water and he beats his tail wildly against the wall where he's lying. If only people were that easy.

Monkey Pod's limp cleared up within a week—some clue that he might have fallen or that he had been running for quite some distance and was just exhausted. I managed to clear up his mange, fed him some coat oil, and his hair stopped coming out in clumps. I got him a cortisone shampoo and flea dip and he has stopped itching and chewing. It was fun to have someone to buy treats for. Could this be a substitute for a boyfriend or perhaps a boyfriend-training device? He came into my life at a time when I so desperately needed a friend, and I was thrilled to have the company.

Unfortunately, there is some sad news to report about Monkey Pod. I took him to the vet for shots and tests and they discovered that he has mature heartworms that are reproducing in gothic proportions of 14" long, spaghetti-sized worms—already lodged in his heart. I looked in the microscope to see the microfilaria twittering about in his blood. His previous owners didn't have the good sense to give him heartworm prophylactics in a place where if you don't treat your dog, he will have worms.

There is some treatment once the host is infested, but the grotesque nature of the worms pales compared to what can happen when you poison the blood with arsenic and the worm carcasses dislodge from the heart. Their stringy bodies could end up stuck in Monkey Pod's jugular veins, killing him. To even comprehend this makes me sick.

On the surface, Monkey Pod seems perfectly healthy, but alas, he has a death sentence. I'm not going to treat him with arsenic. And now I have begun to piece together a clue about his abandonment: the Humane Society will euthanize any animal that they discover has heartworms. Not wanting to face this reality, someone probably abandoned him rather than leaving him at the Humane Society with the hopes that he would get adopted when in fact he would be put down. I couldn't imagine doing this to him and could not imagine giving him up for adoption for the next unsuspecting foster owner.

So Monkey Pod has a terminal diagnosis, and I have just become his hospice nurse. It seems that I will be learning a few things from this dog about letting go of something I have come to love in the middle of my life and at the end of his.

Yesterday I took Monkey Pod to the Kapoho tide pools for the first time. I have heard that Labs by nature love water and are ardent swimmers. From our visits to the beach, I have not seen this in him. I had to pull him by the collar into the calm tide pool. He wasn't particularly fond of this and actually made a growling noise—to let me know he was being patient with me against his better instincts.

Oh well, I thought, I'm not going to force him. So, I zipped up my wetsuit and attached my mask and fins and dove below into the magical psychedelic underwater world of tropical fish and blue brain corals. Within 30 seconds I felt something crawling onto my back. It was Monkey Pod trying to rescue me! Water came in around the sides of my mask as I smiled. I shot off toward the middle of the tide pool with a kick of my fins and turned to watch from below the water line to see him swimming with his four-legged paddling technique. It reminded me of the film *The Black Stallion,* seeing the horse swimming on a tropical island.

Monkey Pod came along quite fast as I moved through a school of raccoon butterflyfish. Then he set out in front of me toward the other bank. He could out-swim me, even with my fins on. So I grabbed his tail and went for a ride.

Monkey Pod pulls me along through the cool blue waters. I hold his tail like a child holds a balloon. We glide over the brain coral beds and past the yellow tangs and black surgeonfish with the orange spots. He's instinctively taking me safely to shore, caring for the only one who has taken the risk to care for him. I'm holding on tight for this wondrous ride of mortals. His paws take hold of the lava rock and soon I will have to let go.

Love, Seaweed

PS—The house, oy vey, the house. The last two weeks have been hellish. The second floor went up quickly, like the first one. Joists first, then platforms and scaffolding were assembled. Everything was hurricane strapped. Scott and Rowdie measured, snapped lines, and erected the four walls and braced them. They built the stairs with the recycled plastic lumber I special ordered and then the moment I had been waiting a year for—the walk up the stairs to see the view from a standing position on the second floor for the very first time. I grabbed my camera and filmed each step as I walked up them. The ocean came into view revealing white caps off shore. Seeing the vast blue from this new vantage was a peak experience.

The roof was next: It is a split-pitch Balinese-style roof that I designed with my draftsman and had engineered and built at a giant truss plant in Ke'au using computers and lasers for accuracy. Alas, the trusses arrived and were damaged in the process of dropping them at the lot. I videotaped them as they hit the lava with a loud crack, breaking the corners of three of them. The fixes we made to them had to be approved and signed off by the truss engineers in California.

Craning on the roof was continually delayed because of rain. First it was the tail of Hurricane Jova, which passed near the island. Then tropical storm Kenneth dumped two inches of water upstairs—held in by the threshold (what contractors call "the plate"). I arrived to see lumber floating like boats upstairs in the standing water. The holes I had drilled through the sub-flooring had clogged with sawdust. I cleaned them out with a nail and watched the water fall to the first floor for hours.

Scott and Rowdie got sick of the rain and I suspect, took an indoor job elsewhere. When they finally planned to return to my job three days later, their truck broke down en route—another lost day. And then the rusty lumber rack collapsed. Finally the storm passed and they ordered the crane for the roof for the next morning.

The crane arrived as scheduled just after dawn and I watched as the roof was put on to the house like a big sun hat, one truss at a time. Scott, Rowdie, and a cranky gay English worker named Mark stood atop the trusses and nailed down each one as it was craned in from overheard. Several neighbors gathered in the street to admire the shape of the roof with its pointy peak and steep slope that then levels out a bit toward the hips. The roof makes the house, like the hat make the outfit.

Then another few days of rain and another unexplained disappearance of Scott and Rowdie. Though they would not admit it, I was certain they had taken on another building project, and I was going to have to start calling them each morning to entice them to show up. Oh how I love being the cheerleader.

Since no one was showing up at the site, I went on the roof in desperation and finished cutting and nailing in the purlins (the support pieces between the trusses) myself. I was struck by the 3rd floor view of the entire area—this is now the highest man-made point in Seaview—and I could see all the way over the berm to Puna Beach Palisades, the adjacent neighborhood. Knowing that once the roof metal was on and the house was sealed, I would never see this view again; I made panoramic videos of it.

Days later, the crew showed up and began hoisting the corrugated roof metal to the trusses and closing up the house. To help out, and since I oddly have no fear of heights, I got the job of screw-down. I climbed a 20-foot ladder resting on the edge of the roof and stepped up onto the slippery surface. With the pitch I had designed, no wonder no one wanted to do the roof screw-down. They must have thought, "You designed it, you screw it down, dude." Holding on to the transition flashing (at the point where the steep pitch meets the less steep pitch), I inched my way toward the peak of the roof with an awl, hammer, bag of screws, and a battery powered screw gun. I grabbed hold of the ridge cap at the top of the roof and began doing the screw-down myself, punching holes first and then dropping a stainless steel screw into each hole and screwing it in.

I found it amusing to drop a screw and watch it shoot down one pitch, then the other and fly right off over the gutters to fall down two stories. If I didn't keep three points of contact and step gingerly on the previous row of screws for traction, I would follow the same trajectory. Fortunately I didn't, and so far, the 20 or so people who have built this house have all left in one piece without injury. I'm very thankful for this.

The last patch of sky visible from inside was shut out and I screwed down the last roof panel. That afternoon, with the roof fully screwed down, the house went dry. In one day, the construction went from looking like a massive, wet jungle gym to a shelter with shade and protection from the rain. It was starting to look like a house.

On the unfinished lanai late in the afternoon after the contractors are gone for the day, I remove my dirty earplugs, turn off the boom box, and rest on boards just listening to the wind and the rain on the roof. I think about the joy that this view will bring me. And I think and hope it will be worth it. For now, I'm just grateful for the dry.

13

September 4, 2005

DR. JEKYLL AND MR. NEW AGE

Day Ninety-One

Doubtful are the words, and dark are the ways,
but in Thy words and ways is light.
Thus then, now as ever, I enter the path of darkness,
if haply so I may attain the light.
—Aleister Crowley

I hate yard work. There, I've said it. I signed on to be the caretaker of Don's house for six months in exchange for a place to stay. But after three months I can no longer disguise that I'm pretty much over it. Caretaking two lots of lawn and gardens in a tropical climate where the grass grows about a foot each week is a part time job. The house construction (a *full* time job) has been wearing on me, and actually, I hate most everything these days. I hate pulling weeds. I hate dragging fallen palm fronds to the frond pile. I hate taking the trash to the dump. I hate filling propane tanks for the refrigerator. I hate hauling all drinking and cooking water. I hate driving 34 miles for a goddamn cookie.

I am by nature cranky; some would even say negative, dark, inching daily toward bitter. Really, the only thing that brings me joy is complaining and listening to Rufus Wainwright singing his dark little songs. It is the rub of the idealist: everything is a little disappointing for someone who expects so much. For me life is simply too harsh, a little too much work, a little too … well it doesn't even matter what something is too much of. And if it's not too much, it's too little.

But what do I have to complain about? The ancient Hawaiians were severely penalized for the smallest infractions of their "kapu" system: crossing or letting one's shadow land on the path of a chief, for example. The penalty was death in most cases—being burned at the stake, clubbed, or speared. By comparison, I don't have all that much to complain about, really.

And nor should most of the new dwellers in the Puna Coast of Hawaii. We have everything that those stuck in their corporate cubicles only dream of. We live in Hawaii, after all—America's tropical dreamland for the newly wed and nearly dead. Our houses flow with warm ocean breezes, we eat fresh fruit off the trees, we go to yoga in the late morning after ecstatic dance at Kalani, then massage in the afternoon, and then hula class, or Dolphin Dance (a form of aquatic bodywork) in the evening. We never shovel snow and never wait for the subway in the freezing cold. Hell, it's the goddamned garden of evil … I mean Eden.

With all these indulgences, why are there so many miserable people here? Why are people beating each other up, doing crystal (here they call it "ice") and screaming like lunatics in the jungle? The answer is simple: they have not learned how to follow their bliss like me, transforming the ugly and mundane into the beautiful and glamorous. Beauty and glamour is really what life is all about, and hey man, if you haven't transformed yourself, you are doomed to be screaming in the jungle.

Like I said, I hate yard work. I have not mowed a lawn since I was 15 years old when I got excused from the chore for being allergic to the grass. I'm 41 now and have cultivated careers that assured me that I would never have to do anything so physical and mundane as cutting grass. I have won the Edward R. Murrow Award for journalism, hosted a national public radio show, and made a short film that is showing around the country and now what do I do to earn my keep? I mow a lawn. The mower smells of exhaust. It's loud. I slip and fall and get filthy and sweaty and I mow over poor lizards whose wiggly parts come flying out all over. Mowing is not beautiful or glamorous, and I cannot wear fabulous footwear or fashion eyewear. In short, it is *not* for effete homos like me.

And yet, here I am in Hawaii caretaking a house whose duties include keeping the lawn mowed and garden beds (full of millipedes) weeded. I have learned that the only way for me to endure this assault on my senses is to transform it. Transformation is the ethos of Puna and so I would like to tell you about how I have devised ways to excite myself about a day of hell on earth—mowing day:

First, I schedule it. I write it down on a piece of paper as an item to be checked off. I even put it in the computer so that I have two places to check off. Then I complain about it wildly. I let everyone know that I can't go snorkeling (one thing I *don't* hate) because I have to mow the lawn. Making a martyr out of myself is useful as well.

Then, I chant about it to myself in the morning. I make up songs by putting my drudgery to music, like the Brahms Lullaby. Feel free to sing it:

Mow the lawn. Mow the lawn.

Now you better get going.
Pull the cord now, do it right now, are you waiting for Pele?
Do it now, and be done and then you can go snorkeling.
Mow the lawn, pull the weeds, welcome to Ha-wa-ii.

And so every other Saturday in Kehena Beach Estates, as dawn breaks, I begin my ramp-up to the great green turf. I psych myself up: To start I am Snoopy in the Sopwith Camel. I snap on my swimming goggles for protection from flying lizard bits. I lick my earplugs (for lubrication) and push them into my brain. Then I'm Janis Joplin and don my psychedelic hot pants and my straw hat. I spray on a primer coat of sunscreen and a mosquito repellant top-coat. I place a tall glass of cool water on the railing near the house and cover it so mosquitoes won't have laid larvae in it by the time I return. I uncover it one more time and take a long swig. I swirl it around, admire the variegated banana tree and the peach-colored abutilons. Oops, I'm stalling.

Then I become Richard the Lionheart on the Third Crusade. I kiss Monkey Pod on the head and with a dramatic farewell, I'm off to battle Saladin in the Holy Land or on the purely mundane terms of my life: an overgrown lawn.

I check my watch—it's 9:30 am. I push up the creaky garage door and wheel out the old lawnmower like an old biplane out of a hangar. I squeeze the throttle three times. "Contact!" I throw the choke and pull the cord and shiver with glee as it sputters into a start with just one yank. A disgusting blue cloud of smoke fills the air. And then I'm off to the back lot with the two front wheels in the air to keep the blade off tree roots along the way.

I insist on starting at the top and working my way downhill in an orderly fashion. If we cannot have glamour, we will have order. Sweeping from side to side, I carve out the most perfect lines. I mow forward and then walk backward pulling the noisy claptrap behind me, rather than mowing to one side and then turning around. This way I can cut the clippings even finer on the second pass. No unsightly windrows will occur on my watch.

About an hour into it, I have reached nirvana. I am one with the trusty lawnmower, which has now picked up several hitchhiking slugs for company. My inner crank is zapped into a Zen-like enlightenment, free of worldly constraints. I am completely dedicated to making this grass the most beautiful patch on earth and yet in a true enlightened state, I am unattached to the outcome.

My body is vibrating in concert with the machine. Inside I am quiet and still. The 2.5 hours it takes to mow becomes the shortest 2.5 hours of the week. I can't wait to meet my holy green master again next week.

I have transformed myself from a miserable, whining, middle-aged Mary with entitlementitis into a humble servant of the mundane. I have successfully transformed my dread into bliss. When I am done mowing, my chakras are vibrated wide open and my kundalini is buzzing. My chi is balanced and my energy is blissful. I am a Puna New Age Bliss Ninny! And I am not alone.

You see, people in coastal Puna are mostly folks who left California's clogged freeways and jam-packed suburbs for the Big Island, funding their tropical early retirement with their real estate gains. In California, pressure and competition kept their minds sharp and ready to face the challenges of high taxes and overcrowding. The Princes of Bavaria I call them—agile creatures, ready to prove their manhood by jockeying their late model German sedans into the closest parking spot at Whole Foods. They might have had a meditation practice or gone to hot nude yoga class three times a week, but at least they had a focus—a job, a real life. Oh, but not here.

When these dilettante seekers of bliss set sail on their golden parachutes bound for Hawaii's shores, they never landed. They lost their focus somewhere about twelve feet off the ground and there they remain hovering just slightly out of reach, stuck in a holding pattern of narcissistic levitation, unable to touch or feel the grounding energies of which they so fervently speak.

These are the people I call the bliss ninnies, the white light Nazis. They are my Puna neighbors. *Punatics,* they're called, heralded on bumper stickers like "Doing My Part to Keep Puna Weird." In California they were the tree huggers. Now they're the dolphin chasers and you can see them coming on the Red Road. They drive really fast: "Get out of my way, dammit, I'm late for my chi gong class!" They speak their own language with lots of "brothers," "energy" and "blessed-be's" thrown in.

Yesterday I was having lunch at the farmer's market with a man who is still in his golden parachute, waiting for clearance for landing. He was talking to me about Alan Greenspan's prediction that the real estate bubble is about to burst and how that might mean he'll sell his small house in California for $800,000 instead of a million. "And I'm OK with that, yep," he said, trying to convince himself.

Meanwhile across the table, two young women with that glow that most of us achieve only after a good fucking are staring into each other's eyes and saying goodbye.

"Well, I'm off to the mainland," the one chick says.

"Gee, that seems so far away," the other replies wistfully.

"Yeah it does. So far away."

"Thank you for being the goddess in my life."

"We're both goddesses."

"Yes, we're reflections of each other." And they smiled, hugged, and parted.

Meanwhile, my friend is going on about maybe splitting the California property into two and thereby realizing a greater return because the sum of two properties is greater than the whole. And what to do with the Honolulu condo and the restraining order on his ex who wants his share of another speculation property. It was exhausting just to listen to it all.

Meanwhile, back at the grassy temple of mowed perfection, I switch off the engine and walk up the back of the lawn to admire my good work. That's part of being a bliss ninny—you must admire yourself endlessly. Writing self-assuring aphorisms on your mirror is an effective way to remind yourself that you are indeed, "the one I've dreamed of for a million years" as an on-line chat encounter recently wrote me about *himself*. It shouldn't have been surprising that he never called when I gave him something so tangible as my phone number. I guess it was too disorienting for him. Hell, if you've been dreaming about yourself for a million years, let's face it, dialing the telephone is just going to seem so outside yourself.

I sat quietly with Monkey Pod (who is an Enneagram 7—The Enthusiast), looking out over the lawn and indulging myself in admiration when I heard the bells ringing. Oh no the bells. Not the bells! Then the horrible voice breaks into some gibberish song. It's the New Age nightmare in the saffron house across the street. He painted his three-story house the color of Hare Krishna robes.

Every morning he rings a bell and then chants (out of key) at full-throttle for the whole neighborhood to hear. After he does this for hours, you'd think he'd be so blissed-out that nothing would bother him. Think again. On a good day you hear bells and the wretched chanting. On a bad day you hear the likes of, "Get out of my house you goddamn *whore!* You fucking *cunt,* get the fuck out of my house and take your bad energy with you, you *bitch."* You get the idea. (Sorry for the expletives, Mom, just reporting the facts.)

Then the girlfriend is usually seen squealing out of the driveway in her pickup truck mowing down his perfectly manicured, exotic blue ginger plants and leaving tread marks all over his lawn. It's a scene repeated again and again in Puna: a New Ager has just bust a vein and look out folks, the golden parachute has landed. Someone just got real and it's not pretty.

Monkey Pod and I sit wincing in the lot below listening to this man's dark side catching up with his bell ringing and we just hope that the girlfriend can navigate her car safely to aroma therapy class for some healing—lavender is very calming, I hear.

And so I've come to realize by comparison that complaining is indeed good for the soul. If you have not complained lately, give it a try. It invigorates the mind and keeps you open to more disappointment. And remember, suffering is grace. By this definition, I live a quiet life of grace here in Puna. I complain for forty minutes each morning and I don't even have to go down the road and pay $12 to do it with people with names like Peace and Spirit.

At 41, I am cranky from stem to stern. Complaining is my spiritual path and the only difference between the New Agers and me is that I admit that I'm miserable. For I have seen my neighbors and now I have seen the light: *Religion is for those who fear going to hell. Spirituality is for those who have been there.*

My mirror and I are reflections of each other.

Aloha, Seaweed Bliss Crank

PS—Hoooo-weee the house is going up fast now. Four walls, two floors, three months of construction and we're less than half way there, my friends now tell me. Whatever happened to that little grass shack in Kealeakekua? I wanna go back.

14

September 27, 2005

IF YOU HAD WINGS

Day One Hundred Fourteen

We revel in these tropic days of transcendent glory, in the balmy breath which just stirs the dreamy blue, in the brief, fierce crimson sunsets, in the soft splendour of the nights, when the moon and stars hang like lamps out of a lofty and distant vault, and in the pearly crystalline dawns, when the sun rising through a veil of rose and gold, rejoices as a giant to run his course, and brightens by no pale gradations into the perfect day.
—Isabella Bird, *Six Months in the Sandwich Islands,* 1875

Sitting at the computer late at night in the cool, darkened house in the jungle, listening to the rain dripping from the trees onto the roof and the sounds of the surf and the little chirps of night creatures in the woods, I've been asking myself why there is so much fascination with Hawaii? I suppose just that short list above would be enough to account for some of the mystique surrounding the Hawaiian Islands, but Florida offers all of that, doesn't it? So might your summer vacation in Hilton Head, Myrtle Beach or Rehoboth.

But if you call the airlines and ask them what the number one desti- nation for frequent flyer award travel is, the answer is this lonely string of volcanic mountains towering over a tectonic hot spot in the middle of the Pacific Ocean from which I write you.

Cozying up to my computer for an evening of writing, I reach into my already opened bag of Pepperidge Farm Mint Brussels to help myself to the last "distinctive cookie" and instead pull out a distinctive dead roach. This reminds me that I have to dig a little deeper to find the charms of Hawaii—you won't find the roaches and some of the other unsightly features of Hawaii on postcards and in tour books. So what is the allure?

The first time I arrived in Hawaii, it was to visit Kauai in 1989. I had just finished having sex with the off-duty flight attendant under a blanket tent when the captain asked the flight attendants to pre- pare for landing. For us, this meant stashing the soiled blanket quickly beneath the seat while simultaneously zipping up and put- ting our tray tables in the upright position and our dicks in the downright position. Only a seasoned slut can handle this three- point move without calling any unwanted attention to himself.

In my flush afterglow, I threw open the window shade and caught my first glimpse of something green—something other than the deep blue Pacific that we had seen for the last several hours. I can only imagine how the first sight of the lavish excesses of green must have seemed to those who sailed to the islands borne on trade winds, or those who navigated outrigger canoes from Polynesia with only the stars for guidance. The first sight of the Hawaiian Islands, however you arrive, is indeed breathtaking.

That sight of verdant "pali" (cliffs) scraping up toward the jet caused a stir in the cabin. The excitement was palpable. It inspired in me a sense of hope—that after this long journey, whatever finan- cial and logistical hurdles I had overcome to get here, finally I would find my piece of paradise. Or at least there was the hope of it.

Dropping in from the sky, it's easy to forget that the nearest land mass is 2,600 miles away, nearly the distance between California and New York. But those who spent months at sea in search of this place must have been moved to tears to focus their watery eyes finally on greens, oranges, browns—to hear the sounds of surf breaking close to shore, tropical birds, the smells of fragrant flowers. I imagine their eyes fixed on the cliffs and the jungles gently rocking into view as they approached the beach. Indeed, to get a true sense of the miracle of these islands sprung up in the middle of nowhere, one must come here by ship, thereby starving you for land.

Isabella Bird wrote of this as her broken-down steamer pulled into Honolulu:

> *There were lofty peaks, truly grey and red, sun-scorched, and wind-bleached, glowing here and there with traces of their fiery origin; but they were cleft by deep chasms and ravines of cool shade and entrancing greenness, and falling water streaked their sides—a most welcome vision after eleven months of the desert sea …*

Nearly everyone who comes to Hawaii today arrives at the Honolulu airport. Their first breath of island air is filled with the cigarette smoke of desperate nicotine addicts standing in the open-air terminal sucking in their airborne vice. Then you make your way to the inter-island terminal via the noisy "wiki-wiki" bus. Isabella Bird's Hawaii it is not. Nonetheless, I was captivated.

Coming from California, the humidity was the first thing that struck me. It set off in me a series of instinctive impulses, the first of which was to shed all my clothes and run naked through the terminal in search of a waterfall and a beach. Aided by the sedative that I tossed back somewhere over the ocean, I was able to resist this urge and proceed to the inter-island terminal in perfect compliance with America's decency laws, though I certainly had flouted them on the plane with the flight attendant. Waterfalls would have to wait. Once you're past the smoking section, the intoxication of that first whiff of untainted Hawaiian air cannot be denied—its fragrance excites the desires of all who come here.

One cannot imagine Biblical parables like that of *Genesis* and the Garden of Eden occurring in a cold place. Adam and Eve shoveling snow? Sorry, that simply wouldn't do. They would have taken to quarreling, "Well I'm sorry Evie, darling, you just shovel your own damn path to that bare apple tree." And so Adam's duties of siring the human race would sadly have come to an end quibbling in a blizzard. The moral implications could hold no weight if the Garden of Eden were a cold and miserable place. Paradise was needed to teach us a good lesson that something beautiful was lost, and now we are doomed to shovel snow in Baltimore for the rest of our mortal lives.

One can, however, imagine such simplistic ideals of the genesis of mankind occurring in Hawaii. The tropics call forth in us a primal instinct to wander naked, eat from the trees, and make babies. Hawaii, for all practical purposes, is as close to the Garden of Eden as one will find on earth. Why else would so many honeymoons be staged here? It isn't because of the roaches, I assure you. And it's not because of cheap airfare, either. It is heeding the call to our origins, a chance to act on instinct, to feel immortal, to find Eden and stand under a waterfall with fresh, cool water flowing from the mountains in a primeval jungle.

Alas, you probably will never stand at the base of that waterfall, real or imagined, because the weight of the waters would crush your body. And if that didn't kill you, the temperature of the water would give you hypothermia leaving you paralyzed in a cold pool of pristine water. Besides, you probably would never allow yourself to run naked down the beach and risk getting a ticket for public indecency thanks to the European missionaries who set the moral tone for the islands in the 19th century. Even if you're from Missouri and you're only going to see it from the window of a $200 helicopter tour, at least you know the waterfall is there and that the part of you that desires to return to an ancient primordial existence, even for a moment, still calls to you. Searching for paradise is coded in your DNA.

If you're that newlywed couple from Missouri, as you return to your surf and turf dinner at the three-star hotel with manicured garden and tiki torches, you fall into your freshly-made bed, your face kissed by the sun—it feels damn good. It feels good to be cradled in the luxury your mainland life has afforded you here. But that scenario is Hawaii like Disney's Epcot Center is the world. It is an American fantasy brought to you in living color like a Disney film, with the coconuts neatly cut out of the trees so as not to conk the bride on the head and incur a catastrophic lawsuit for the hotel chain.

This uniquely American construct—sanitized for your protection—is one that the average tourist will likely never stray from, barring doing something stupid like getting caught in a snow storm on the summit of Mauna Kea in their aloha shirts and slippahs and being sent to the hospital with frostbite. Otherwise, they simply won't have the opportunity to see behind the bamboo-print curtains to the inner workings of Hawaii.

The other side of the predictable tropical vacation fantasy is in fact, the other side of the island: the wet side—the side that gets 15 *feet* of rain each year. Hilo, for example, the state's second largest city, is a working city not solely for the benefit of tourists. It is a charming old whaling and sugar shack town—the county seat of the island of Hawaii. It is the original tourist destination of the Big Island, before it all packed up and moved to Kona, leaving Hilo's decidedly Japanese middle class to the rain.

Further south of Hilo (and a little bit toward outer space), lies the Puna district, the place where I am building my home. *Here* one can really see what lurks behind those bamboo-print curtains, and it isn't always pretty: Puna has long been the dumping ground of Hawaii, an open-air asylum of sorts. It couldn't accurately be considered the inner "workings" of Hawaii, because practically no one here works. Nonetheless, it is strangely refreshing. It's gritty and unseen by the throngs who jet into Kona and plop down on the beach in search of a predictable vacation.

Puna's capricious weather and the wild and colorful castaways in primer-gray cars without hubcaps are the very reason I am able to afford to build here, though if the community were more interesting and the real estate were cheaper, I too would likely be on the dry side of the island. Tourists don't like rain and they definitely don't like weirdoes spoiling their well-earned holiday.

On any given day, Seaview trots out its regular cast of characters: the lady who takes her pet macaws for a fly, chasing them on her little red scooter claiming that parrots are smarter than dolphins; the white guy with dreads down to his waist who believes he's one of Jesus' disciples and will ask you to "butt fuck me in the ass" [*sic*] at the beach; the dolphin lady who names all the dolphins she swims with and claims that one of them is trying to get it on with her; the guy who lives in the notorious house of cards—built with scraps of plywood nailed willy-nilly together to form a mishmash of leaning trapezoids stacked atop each other that he claims is appraised at $2,000,000; the screamer who is a heroin addict and who robs houses taking only food; the woman who has her pants pulled up to her boobs and commands her dogs in German (she doesn't speak German but figures that because the dogs are German shepherds, they'll understand the commands better in their native language. Nein! Plotz!); Yellin' Helen who is famous for belting out lines in the middle of the night like, "Any woman who tells you she likes it up the ass is lying! I mean, isn't my pussy tight enough?"; the naked notary; the guy who drives with his left foot out the window; the guy who drives a motorcycle with his dog on the front; the surfer boys who play ukulele on the roof. I could go on ad infinitum.

I don't know, maybe macaws *are* smarter than dolphins, and maybe dolphins *do* do try to get it on with people. Call me boring, but really, I'd rather just have pleasant dinner conversation and get it on with someone from my own species.

Colorful as it is, this is no Disney film with requisite happy ending. Living in this haole ghetto in Puna has gone a long way to deflate my island fantasy balloon. I was kinda hoping for a nice platter of pupus and a tropical drink with a cocktail umbrella at the beach. Now I actually kinda like that contrived spirit of aloha that I find on the dry side of the island. Sometimes I think I would prefer to just stay safely in my fantasy world, which is damn near impossible in Puna.

If you remember the now extinct Disneyworld Tomorrowland ride *If You Had Wings,* you might recall it was Eastern Airlines' glamorous portrayal of our planet-as-playground. So long as you had a passport and could afford their airfare, the world was your oyster. But for those too poor to travel, (and for those who don't really like oysters), there was at least this ride. It was free—no ticket required, only your brand loyalty was expected.

If you stepped into the blue bucket chairs that slowly glided along a track for a four-and-a-half-minute fantasy ride around the globe while choruses of women sang in your ears in stereo, you would have seen projections of cliff divers and people cavorting on tropical beaches, in waterfalls and rainforests. Humidity was added to the air for effect. A cloud projector simulated a moonlit night sky all while birds projected on the rounded walls flapped their way through the course of the ride with you. It was a brilliant construct of all that sparkles in paradise. At 13, I was determined to some day escape the dumpy confines of East Fort Myers and find that idyll.

I confess that I came to Hawaii riding a wave of my own personal idealism. I now know that I was looking for my very own Eastern Airlines ride. Or was it the *Enchanted Tiki Room,* or *Gilligan's Island?* There are no Disney rides depicting Tucson, Arizona. Seduced by the warm trade winds and temperate climate, I came to the island thinking that somehow I would be happier than I was in Tucson with its less-than-charming desiccating winds and urban sprawl.

Alas, Hawaii is like anywhere else—if you come here an emotional mess and think that that the balmy breezes will give you a Disney ride back to mental health, I hate to be the one to disappoint you. They won't. If you come to Hawaii thinking that everything will be better, that you'll fall in love, and you'll swim in warm mountain pools and phosphorescent bays, that dolphins will hump you, and you'll never have to worry about the mundane in life, you'll end up slack-jawed and stoned-out on Kehena Beach complaining about Wal-Mart and wishing you could afford your airfare back while your guitar busts its seams in the salt air. *Twang.* I offer this sermon as much to myself as to anyone.

Making peace with Puna has meant acknowledging that the vacation is over, that Gilligan is dead and that an admittedly less glamorous life has begun here. It is a life set before an excessively beautiful backdrop that keeps me somewhat drugged-out: "Oooh pretty! My health insurance doesn't cover me in Hawaii. But, Oooh pretty! Must take the maggoty trash out. But, Oooh pretty! Just ran over a mongoose, stepped on a cane toad, and ate a roach carcass in my ice cream. But, Oooh pretty!"

Sometimes while I'm driving the Red Road, I notice the Pride of Aloha cruise ship sailing toward Kilauea to see molten lava pouring into the ocean just before the passengers gorge themselves at the midnight buffet. It makes me smile watching this city of lights silently moving along the coast with little sparks of flash bulbs pricking the darkness. It reminds me that people come from all the over the world and pay a very high price to see what I could walk to. This is their once in a lifetime dream vacation and I sit here amid my crazy neighbors arguing. I listen to yelling in the jungle while the passengers snarf mousse tartlets by the ice sculptures.

Tonight I stepped outside onto Don's lanai to comfort Monkey Pod, who was cowering from my tirade with a flyswatter against an invasion of the 82nd Airborne Division of flying roaches from the jungle. I noticed the sky. The coconut palm trees were silhouetted against the moon as clouds moved quickly in the dark sky, caught briefly in the accusatory gray light. It looked wonderfully familiar and so perfect that it seemed artificial. It was as if some underground technician at Disney was orchestrating my vision. Cue the sound of the ocean crashing. Cue the passing rain shower. It *is* the *Tiki Room* and it *is If You Had Wings.* The flowers are crooning and I am in the blue bucket seat twisting and turning while the chorus is singing, *"If you had wings, you could do many things. You could widen your world. If you had wings, had wings, had wings."*

The ride was dismantled and unceremoniously thrown into the trash in 1987. Eastern Airlines went out of business in 1991 and Gilligan (Bob Denver) died a couple weeks ago at age 70. Aloha, Little Buddy.

Paradise, I have grudgingly learned is not some Disney ride or sophomoric TV show. It is found in the quiet of a walk with Monkey Pod to the mailbox along the guava-stained road. He sniffs and pees and I complain about having to carry home junk mail.

Love, Seaweed

PS—What does it take to find an electrician in Hawaii? Do I have to climb Kilauea and get on my hands and knees? I'm willing if that's what it takes. I'll wear my kneepads, though.

I've spent several weeks chasing down leads for an electrician, each one escaping my grasp—they were too booked or wouldn't even return my calls. Finally, I came up with a company that was well recommended and big enough that they could squeeze me in: Moke's Electric from Hilo. I drove into town and left blueprints on Moke's doorstep. His wife called me back with a staggering estimate of almost $7,000 to wire the house—*not* including any of the light fixtures, dimmers, or fans. This was twice what I had expected, but typical of building here, you take what you can get.

I paid my deposit on the electric work and then waited for them to show up. Week after week of delays. Each day I would call and they would tell me they'd be out tomorrow and then come up with some great excuse why they didn't show. I heard everything from "The truck broke down on the saddle road," to "Our driver got a ticket and had to go to court," to "We had an emergency job in Honolulu." There must be a book of contractor's excuses that is sold at the checkout counter at Home Depot. So I have gone on without the electricians for now. I just hope I haven't lost my deposit in a scam.

The plumbing is well under way. Drainpipe's staff is incredibly pleasant to work with—friendly, knowledgeable, and efficient. They're tearing up the house, drilling holes in the frame, dripping molten solder on the slab (which they swear will come up), and running copper supply lines throughout the house.

Meanwhile, on the leeward side of the house, I wear my earplugs, big straw hat, and slippahs painting trim boards glossy white and the siding celery green. I guess I was supposed to sand the trim first—the finish was a little rough. Scott tisked-tisked me while taking a drag off his cigarette one afternoon. I half expected him to tap his ashes onto my wet paint and make me lick it off. My self-esteem takes quite a beating on a daily basis. Building this house is like construction boot camp, and I'm the dumb recruit, a bit like Private Benjamin. Scott is the drill sergeant, only I'm paying his salary and supposed to be *his* boss. The tail is clearly wagging the dog.

15

October 18, 2005

LEAPING LAKES OF LAVA

Day One Hundred Thirty-Five

Each evening, after a hard day of construction, comes my favorite part of the day: a trip to Kalani Honua to use the pool and hot tub. My hot, soapy shower has become a ritual cleansing of the day's stresses and toxins. After showering, I slip into the pool and swim a few gentle laps under the stars while my mind churns through the day's events. Then I spend a half-hour or so in the hot tub visiting with staff that I have befriended while my body unknots and I pick the paint out of my arm hairs.

Last night I invited my Seaview neighbor Bill along. He has become my closest friend and building advisor. He's an interesting mix of small town Ohio (he pronounces it Ahah), big city lawyer, island hippie, bitchy queen, massage therapist, and father of two. He also built his own home and shows up at my site almost daily to give me words of encouragement.

Driving home from Kalani after sitting in the hot tub for a couple of hours listening to some guy yammer on about his Zoloft regimen, Bill and I were remarking about the moon. The moon here has such significance in our lives because we're so remote. Far from any city light pollution, and so far out to sea, the moon turns the nights into a silvery evening playground for a few days each month. We drove along the Red Road toward Seaview looking back over our shoulders to catch the moon shimmering over the ocean. Suddenly I had the good sense to look in the direction of the motion of the car for once and shrieked, "Wow, look at the volcano!" The clouds in the sky hovering over Kilauea were aglow with orange like we had never seen before.

That particular shade of orange seen at night turns my blood cold, sending shivers up and down my spine. There's an instinctive impulse to grab my possessions and head for the hills—well in the case of a volcanic emergency, heading for the hills wouldn't really be all that smart. OK, into the lifeboats then.

In 1993, living in the Lower Haight of San Francisco, back when it wasn't even vaguely trendy, I awoke to that very shade of orange that forever set my conditioned response to flee. It was the day after Thanksgiving at about four in the morning when I heard the sirens. In the Haight, sirens are not really all that unusual. It's when the whirring stops nearby and then you hear the sounds of the diesel engines revving up to pump water that you should become concerned. It did just that and I freaked out. I flew out of bed, cranked open the vertical blinds in the back of the house to see the sky full of airborne orange sparks and the backs of buildings reflecting that shimmering orange color I have come to dread.

I threw on my clothes, woke my housemate Ed and ran up onto the roof. From there we could see the spreading blaze destroying several Victorian houses just a block away. We ran down to the street and witnessed the horror of a post-Thanksgiving meltdown with hippies in the street in their underwear screaming at the fire-fighters to do something while the water spray from their hoses kept failing. Flames walked through walls like orange ghosts. An ornate Victorian turret dropped onto a car below in a big molten plop. In the end, the blaze took out seven buildings. For me, it was the beginning of the end of my fascination with sketchy neighborhood living. I fled the Lower Haight to the more civilized Noe Valley. My life has become increasingly less inner-city since.

The Big Island of Hawaii contains the most active volcano on earth and for someone concerned about fire, it's probably not the best choice of locales. In 1875, Isabella Bird put it this way when she stood at the edge of the orange lake Hale-mau-mau (house of everlasting fire):

> *I think we all screamed, I know we all wept, but we were speech-less, for a new glory and terror had been added to the earth. It is the most unutterable of wonderful things. The words of common speech are quite useless … here was the real 'bottomless pit'—'the fire which is not quenched'—'the place of hell'—'the lake which bur-neth with fire and brimstone'—the 'everlasting burnings' the fiery sea whose waves are never weary.*

Bird was overcome with the emotion of seeing something that she couldn't have seen on the Discovery Channel. She *was,* after all, the Discovery Channel and the *National Geographic* of her time. My first sight of the lava was a little more circumspect. I knew what to expect.

But seeing the orange in the sky last night meant that maybe that fiery lake that burneth was about to runneth into my neighborhood. I began to whine to Bill, "But my house isn't insured yet, it can't erupt now." My mind was having hot flashes of seeing that river of fire flowing down my street melting through pavement and houses in its path, as it has done before. I swear after all I have been through building the house, that if that were the case, I'd go for a little dip in the orange specter rather than face the desecration of a dream.

Bill and I raced toward the glowing clouds to investigate. Telephone poles were silhouetted against the glowing sky like the scene in *Gone with the Wind* with Atlanta burning in the background. We drove past Seaview and Puna Beach Palisades, both built on 1955 lava flow; past Kehena Beach Estates—a lush green neighborhood spared from the rivers of fire 50 years ago. We drove on past the charred black pahoehoe of Kaimu and Kalapana, both ravaged by lava from 1989–1991.

Kalapana consisted of a tiny town and Kaimu an idyllic black sand beach with palm trees lining the shore. Now there are only a few houses and many square miles of cooled lava. No more little town. No more palm trees. No more sand. No more surfing—just miles of black silence. It seems like the handiwork of an irate god. That is unless you have come to realize as I have, that the jungle is a little less than fabulous and that lava provides something that Hawaii has so precious little of: open space. To come and sit in the middle of a vast pile of black cinder is the cure for jungle fever, jungle rot, and the curse of the creepy crawlers. It's also a great place for naked photo-shoots—human flesh looks great against a backdrop of black.

Miraculously, at the end of the Red Road, in the middle of this sea of twisted licorice-like basalt is a kipuka containing Verna's restaurant, a kava bar, and the local home of the Hawaiian sovereignty movement. "Kipuka" in Hawaiian means an opening—usually referring to a patch of land that has not been ravaged by lava. It is an oasis amid the destruction. Kipukas are usually old-growth mangos, avocados, palms, and tangles of vines tying it all up into a neat little package of green. This is one of the most famous kipukas in Hawaii—the home of Uncle Robert and his extended family.

Reading Queen Liliuokalani's biography: *Hawaii's Story,* you can begin to understand why Hawaiians call each other Uncle and Auntie so freely. The "alii" (royalty) freely adopted children based on their whim—commoners bearing a child did not come with any entitlement to actually raising the child, nor did they want to as such. It was an early version of the concept "it takes a village." It would seem more logical then, to invent several Uncles and Aunties instead of mothers and fathers. It's a term of endearment and reverence and Uncle Robert's family is indeed a revered one, a treasure of the Puna district.

The large and avuncular Robert (whose veins flows with rare 100% Hawaiian blood) sits under a shed roof at the edge of his property in a plastic lawn chair and welcomes locals and tourists alike with a kindness that people have come to associate with aloha—that unique artifact of Hawaiian culture which means (among many things) to share. Uncle Robert lives aloha and his compound has a gentle good spirit that one simply can't find readily in American culture.

Here in the kipuka, their family dispenses Hawaiian culture, offering language classes, music, food, and a storyboard of the sovereignty movement, all under an upside-down Hawaiian flag. Foot stencils on the pavement invite you in and signs that say, "Welcome" and "No Shame" greet you. It's very un-American and almost an act of defiance for his family to live with such open generosity after all that has been done to the Hawaiian people by the American government.

Bill and I parked at the end of the road, grabbed our flashlights and headed out onto the lava to get a better view of the lava flow. Stepping over the black slabs and cracks, we headed out toward the ocean over the top of what was once a beach. From there we could see the source of the orange reflection on the clouds—a pond of molten lava had collected at the top of the hill, overflowing into a red hot river toward the ocean where a plume of steam shot into the air and drifted back over the volcano.

My initial fears were quieted seeing that the flow was contained and making its way safely to the sea without touching neighborhoods with its fiery fingers. The pooling lava at the hilltop and the low-lying clouds and steam had reflected the glow and triggered our alarms. It gave the illusion of grave danger when in reality it was nothing more than a fun light show—Hawaii's version of the northern lights. For now, we were spared the dreaded flow.

We head back toward Uncle Robert's. Tonight they're serving ava drinks—a sort of tea made from the kava root that produces a mild euphoria, numbs your lips, tastes like dirt, and keeps you up peeing all night long. The outdoor bar welcomes locals and haoles who come to "talk story," meet friends, and sit spaced-out on ava under the string of colored lights and palm trees. For those of us addicted to *Gilligan's Island* references, the bar looks like a set where Ginger and Mary Ann would be sitting, gossiping about Gilligan's latest antics. Some of Uncle Robert's family come out from time to time and sit at the bar and play slack-key guitar and sing in Hawaiian. On weekends, locals come to play the jungle piano—an old beater of an instrument that twangs and thuds but somehow produces a melody in spite of the dead keys and rusted strings. Others in Uncle Robert's family play the ukulele and the string bass. It's basically the Hawaiian VonTrapp family running around in slippahs in the kipuka.

One of Robert's eleven children is Puna, a gentle-giant gay troubadour. His hair spins out of his wide head in dyed strands of wildness. He speaks in a very high, breathy voice and is both gracious and shy. He advances with a generous aloha greeting and then quickly retreats looking at the ground. Tonight, Puna is standing where the parking lot meets the edge of the lava, under the moonlight with three other gay Hawaiian friends. They speak a mixture of

Hawaiian, pidgin and English. Bill was saying something to me but I committed my ears to listening to Kavika and Puna bantering in Hawaiian. That was the first time I have heard the language used in any casual setting. I was dumbstruck and thrilled to finally hear it.

We told them we came looking for the lava. They spoke about when they were in school together as children in Pahoa, remembering the earthquakes and the rumbles as Kilauea began to erupt. Duane remembered when they left the classroom how they could see the lava shooting up and Puna demonstrated with the red light stick he had just cracked open by holding it on top of his head. We all laughed.

Kavika, who is only 24, was playing a ukulele that he hugged to his chest like a child would hold a stuffed animal, and Duane who was missing a tooth in the front, stood beside a car in the moonlight spontaneously breaking out into hula with an added campy flair. He enjoyed the spotlight of the moon, but when we trained our flashlights on him, he hunkered to the pavement giggling with embarrassment. Puna was singing in Hawaiian with Kavika, and Bill and I were trying to hum the harmonies.

Hawaiian music always seems to be about natural beauty: the colors of the rainbow the mist of a waterfall, a bird flying over the green cliffs of the ocean, or the fragrance of the flowers in the air. We didn't know for sure what the words were, but one thing was certain: they were not singing "bye, bye Miss American Pie," or "a little ditty about Jack and Diane," and they're not singing about beating up fags, or driving a truck and all the other inanities of American pop music. These are gay boys—all just a little queeny, wonderfully goofy and uninhibited here out of view of the lava gazers who don't know enough to head to the end of the road and get out of the car. Because Bill and I are gay and known from our involvement about town we are granted entrée. (It's one of the beauties of gay culture—it affords you immediate access to an underground culture and can serves as a bridge to the indigenous culture in a foreign land that most people will never have access to.)

What touched me the most was that this spontaneous outbreak of Hawaiian culture was not for the tourists. There was no hotel luau and buffet, no poolside torch-lighting ceremony at 6 pm sharp, no woman on a loudspeaker routinely explaining the Hawaiian culture for us in English, and no tip jar. This is life without television—no subtitles or narration, but with a wonderfully soft musical score and improvised dance number. This is the lost language, the culture, the music, the "aikane" (gay), the aloha, and it is alive and crooning about the extraordinary beauty of this land while drinking beer out of the trunk of a car in a parking lot at the edge of the lava. It is gay men upholding a tradition of singing with a simple instrument in delicate falsetto harmonies under the moonlit sky with a splash of orange to the west, and the lights of the kava bar twinkling at the center of Uncle Robert's kipuka.

Bill and I watched the party disappear up and onto the pahoehoe. Puna and Duane twirled their red and green glow sticks in giant circles. They remarked when they cracked them open into color that it looked like Christmas. I could see a rain cloud approaching and darkening the moon. Puna, in his high and delicate voice said, "Aloha guys. Merry Christmas."

Aloha, Seaweed

PS—The exterior of the house is at last done. Last week we had a crew of 13 workers, 4 dogs, 1 child, 2 blaring radios (each tuned to different stations) and me pacing in my straw hat with earplugs in, chewing my nails, and writing checks.

I arrived with Monkey Pod one day and nearly had my ankles chewed by two pig-dogs tied to the back of a contractor's truck. I went over to calm them down and was waved off by Scott, "They're not normal dogs. They're for hunting. Don't go near them!" I had the contractor move his truck so they weren't chasing everyone who came to the site. The contractor, a local, spited me by cheating on his time by $400. At least he did an excellent job installing the Trex decking to perfection. I grumbled at the ethical violation but wrote it off figuring this was my small reparation for the occupation of Hawaii.

The house passed its nailing and shear-wall inspections, and Scott and Rowdie sawed away on the Hardi-Panel until all the siding was up in about one week. Cutting the siding was a dirty and noisy job. It's basically concrete in thin sheets and creates a huge amount of smoke and noise to cut each piece. Then it must be hand-nailed. I hired a couple neighbors to come in and help me with the nailing. We attacked the house with hammers and left smash marks wherever we missed the nails. Later I had to patch and paint them. I now see the beauty of a nail gun as I spent the evenings icing my hammer elbow.

I spent an entire day taking apart the crates that the windows and sliding glass doors were packed in, then earmarking which window went where. I ordered bronze-tinted windows on the east and west sides. My brother Sean suggested I order awning windows for the windward side so they could remain open in the rain. It was a brilliant suggestion. All the windows are now installed and trimmed on the exterior.

The rain gutter people came and installed the seamless ducts and connected them to the water tank. This was a big disaster. They routed the second floor gutters from the roof to the eyebrow (the roof over the first floor doors) that would then drain to the water tank, or so we thought. Alas, after they installed it and it began to fill the tank, we realized that the eyebrow was lower than the top of catchment tank (a cardinal sin) and so when the tank reached about

7,500 gallons, water began to back up over the lip of the eyebrow. The whole system had to be re-designed at my expense.

Aloha Gutters blamed Waterworks for installing the tank too high. Waterworks blamed Aloha for designing the system poorly. In this case I sided with Waterworks because Aloha also put only two downspouts for the entire roof, which in a good downpour meant hundreds of gallons went spilling over the edge. They came back a second time and gave me four downspouts, again at my expense. At least they were friendly and so I bit the bullet and chatted with Roberta as her family climbed, drilled and fixed things. In the end, because of the roof size, it managed to collect more than just glances: over 3,000 gallons of rainwater were captured in just one rainy weekend.

The plumbing rough-in went well. The plumbers even managed to clean things up when they left—something virtually unheard of. They will put in the solar water heater soon and then comes the electric rough-in. I'm hoping Moke's Electric will show up some day.

I spend my days racing around the site trying to put out fires, tame dogs, run errands, make decisions on materials, anticipate contractors' needs, make appointments, get bids for each next step. It's unbelievable how much has to be done.

Hopefully next week we begin sheet rocking and then I get to hand-trowel 4,352 square feet of drywall including a 14-foot ceiling. Gee, then it's painting, flooring, concrete staining, final on the electric and plumbing, appliance installation, and oh forget it … this is just endless.

Come and help paint!

16

December 6, 2005

MISTER ROGERS' NEIGHBORHOOD OF FREAKS

Day One Hundred Fifty-Four

I like you just the way you are. You're special to me.
—Fred Rogers

From what I hear on NPR in the car on those endless supply trips to Hilo, it is late autumn in America—a detail I find hard to believe when it's still hot and steamy here. I guess I get some perverse thrill hearing of people slogging through snow while I'm mopping my sweaty brow and swimming naked in the ocean.

Thanksgiving, the one holiday that I do actually celebrate, sort of passed uneventfully. I had already begun to assemble a list of whom I would and wouldn't sit at the dinner table with. The folks who show up with a half-eaten bag of chips and guacamole (please, no more guacamole), suck down all the wine in short order, get stoned out of their minds, and then babble away about themselves were dropped from my list. With those criteria established, there were very few dinner candidates left. I wanted to be with Bill and my new lesbian friend and fellow-writer Kimberly Dark for the holiday, but Bill wanted to attend a big social event where more than just the turkey was baked. Kimberly is vegan, and the thought of Thanksgiving without cold weather, without autumn leaves, in a place where there's really no celebration of the harvest time because it's always harvest time … well, what *is* it, then? I needed the turkey and stuffing as a seasonal marker. In the end, the three of us had a vegan dinner at Bill's in the afternoon with baked tofu and rice.

But the next day, Kiki, a new lesbian friend who is a miracle-worker in the kitchen, made a fantastic leftovers dinner at her beach house and Bill and I went over and indulged ourselves in a more traditional celebration with turkey, stuffing, mashed potatoes and gravy.

More than a month has elapsed since I last wrote. I've been wondering why that is. Why have I been uninspired to write? Could it be that the novelty of living in America's third world paradise has gone flat? Maybe my initial enthusiasm has mildewed like the red suede shoes that I brought here and have not worn once? I guess I have gotten somewhat used to the beauty of Hawaii, though I wouldn't say that I have taken it for granted or that I've become blasé about it, really. On the contrary, my appreciation for Hawaii was renewed yesterday by just a couple minutes of watching CNN at a friend's house. Plastic correspondents were reporting from the streets of Washington DC wearing ties and make-up and bras—oh my! The women had bleached hair teased into that typical anchor-woman style where it curves around their faces making them look like fancy chickens. All the men are clean-shaven and uptight-looking. It's modern America—something I've not really seen for over six months now. And honestly, at this moment, I think I could live without it. Though, I wouldn't mind visiting a Trader Joe's once in a while.

That sight of people freezing on urban street corners in order to get the story, to get close to that gorilla in the White House who walks as if his hairy arms should be dragging on the ground, well, let's just say it makes my lonely dusk walks with Monkey Pod down a wet jungle road even more sweet than the scent of guavas hanging in the air. I guess if I hadn't spent so many nights in New York City in the snow and rain, I might feel just a twinge of envy for those folks all tied up in bundles waiting for their express trains. But I don't feel that twinge now. If I hadn't seen every opera of the season in San Francisco and New York for years, I might feel a little like a bumpkin here, so far away from it all. But I don't now.

So I guess that's part of the answer why I have not been inspired to write. A small wave of contentment has washed up on my shore, and who can possibly write when they're content? The other part of the answer is that as we finished framing the house and moved inward to refinements that require my presence, I've really had no free time to write. Plus, I haven't really written that much about the details of building because I figure it's mostly mundane and really not that interesting to the non-builders among us, myself included.

The most interesting people do not issue forth to the construction site each day to engage me in conversation about the delicate nuances of Grieg's Fourth Nocturne. No, it's the Knights of Toyota and the Lords of Chaos who arrive each day with dogs in the back and lumber on top. They bring blaring radios and set them atop piles of drywall and debris and go about their days fiddling with tools like Rotozips and Roto Hammers which do things like cut drywall in circles and drill holes in concrete while simultaneously going up and down like a very aggressive lover might screw the daylights out of you. If only.

I embarrass myself asking the wielders of such gadgetry questions that don't use the proper building terminology. I don't speak "Builder." I say things like, "Those beams there are every two feet apart, right?" They say, "The joists are two-feet on-center." Well, I figure, why do we have to say that "on-center" thing? What kind of idiot is going to measure from the left side of one joist to the right side of the next one? (Incidentally I use mnemonic devices like Joyce DeWitt to remember words like "joist.")

So I don't say, "on-center." It's an act of defiance or some form of pride in being not only a haole, but also being a sissy who really knows diddly-squat about building. But, dammit, I'm paying the bills and I'm going to ask dumb questions and do dumb things if I damn well please. For example: there is a 3-inch drainpipe that comes down from upstairs through the bathroom below. It has a cap on it that has a square grip that sticks out beyond the studs (now there's one building term I've had no trouble learning) where the drywall is supposed to hang. So we would have to drywall around it. Well, I had the bright idea to unscrew the inward turned cap and turn it around so that the cap would protrude on the inside of the poop shoot instead of outside and then we could drywall over it. One of the builders frowned at me, "Brah, you can't do that." ("Brah," by the way, is not a contraction of brassiere. It's a pidgin contraction for "braddah," which is a bastardization of brother. In essence, brah is like saying, "bro.") Fearing a backup of my upstairs poo trying to make its way down to the cesspool and getting hung up on the cap, we took the cap off and replaced it with a "flush cap" and promptly drywalled over it. I didn't know such things as flush caps even existed.

Builder speak is a proving ground. Like the tools they lug and the trucks they drive, builders establish a pecking order based on how fast they can download information before your eyes glaze over and you're lost—their desired state for you. If you jump off the conversation lost, expect that they will take you for a ride. But if you can stay with it and know the terminology, then you might stand a chance at being respected, charged properly, and in the end, actually knowing what the hell was done and what to do next.

The other day Scott the tile guy was telling me, "OK, go to the tile store and get the 40-mil rubber underlayment for the shower pan. First, measure the square footage and get a bag of shower pan mix for each 10-square feet, except that the edges are higher up and slope down to the adjustable drain and so you'll need more for that and don't forget to get an extra 6-inches of underlayment for over-hanging the curb." What I heard was the following: Humina humina humina store. Humina humina humina rubber. Humina humina humina shower. Humina humina humina 6-inches. I was fixated on his parted round buttocks while he was on his hands and knees giving me the order. I watched him mesmerized and feckless, thinking of a time when I won't be building when I can return to being my old carefree sexpot self. I have reached a certain level of indolence with what seems like an endless task—this house build-ing—and so my mind wanders, sometimes irretrievably.

I head into Hilo with images in my mind of the tile guy's ample ass crowding out his instructions of what to buy. Not surprisingly, I got the wrong thing. I returned to the job site hours later like Char-lie Brown with insufficient amounts of shower mix and we're nearly 40-miles from the nearest tile store. Fortunately, most of the build-ers who have pranced around my prairie, like to prove themselves by actually being prepared for the inevitable idiot like me. They usually have just what they need in the back of their truck, even though they'll send you on a wild goose chase looking for it. And so he pulls out a half used bag of shower pan mix and now we have a glorious shower pan with a 3/4" slope to the drain. Garsh, it's so pretty I could just lick it. Forget about the tile guy, this shower pan is gorgeous! My drool would easily slide down the perfectly crafted slope and into the drain.

See what I mean? I've gone temporarily insane. Who in his right mind could get interested in this crap? It's a shower pan, for the love of god.

Moke and His Minions

Moke *finally* showed up with his team of amped-up electricians to wire the house. I guess it stands to reason that electricians are the speediest of all the workers. I think because of their constant exposure to electrical current, it leaves them in a perpetual state of being wired. The two days they were there for the electrical rough-in, construction was put on fast-forward.

Moke's "hapa-haole," (part white) son, who works shirtless and speaks both perfect English and pidgin, is the foreman—surly, cute, and competent. His dad comes in only when something major has gone wrong or to meet with the client, and then his staff completely submits to him as if he were a samurai warrior. It was fascinating to see Moke's personal power—their submissiveness was certainly something he has cultivated in them. I half expected to see Moke tying them up to the lanai posts and caning them for their mistakes.

Anyway, Moke's son jumps out of the van and the first thing out of his mouth is, "Where are your fixtures?"

"What fixtures?" I asked with a roll of my eyes and a dramatic exhale. I showed him the boxes of fans and a small mountain of dimmers I had purchased. I was certain that the number of dimmers indicated to him that I was a homosexual. "We *have* to have dimmers everywhere—*especially* in the bathrooms. I'd put them in the *fridge* if I could," I told him with a certain queenly arrogance that I felt entitled to after forking over top dollar for their services. He was not amused.

"Your cans, where are your cans?" He demanded, chewing his gum rapidly and mashing out his cigarette on the ground. I wasn't sure I could chew gum and smoke at the same time. I marveled at his ability not to choke or blow the gum out with the smoke. It all seemed so complicated—chewing and smoking. In my detached state I wondered what smoke-flavored gum would taste like. Or what if the gum got stuck on the cigarette? I've been building too long now to care about these momentary exigencies any more. My insouciance toward the electricians felt well deserved since I had waited for so long for them to show up. Now I wanted to have a lit-tle fun and make *them* squirm.

"I thought *you* supplied those. Here, I'll get that for you," and I bent over and picked up his cigarette butt nodding and flashing him a little smirk without averting my gaze. It was a subtle fuck-you that I'm certain he picked up on. I indeed thought they supplied the housings for the fixtures. Oh dear, not another unexpected expense. When I booked Moke for the job, he was so quick with me on the phone, rattling off all that I needed that I didn't quite grasp this small but important detail.

"No, we don't supply the housings. And we need them now," he told me impatiently. Checkmate. I lose. If I want recessed lighting I'm going to have to go get the housings.

"Well, tell me what you want and I'll run to town and get them," I said with conciliation. He seemed annoyed to have to explain to me what I had to buy. How could someone so cute be such a pain in the ass?

We went over the blueprints, walked through the house and made a list. I rushed into Hilo only to find that Home Depot was entirely out of stock with recessed lighting cans. When I was buying dimmers, I cleaned out their supply. Seems everyone in Southeast Hawaii is doing recessed lighting with dimmers—a real sign that some serious homosteading is going on. I cannot tell you how many times I have been to Home Depot to find they were completely out of stock of the item I was looking for, and, you guessed it—a six week wait for re-supply. Fortunately, the Contractor's Desk referred me to another electrical supply warehouse.

I darted out and managed to find the warehouse and indeed they had all that I needed in stock at twice the cost of Home Depot. I raced back to the job site to deliver the cans. They seemed unimpressed—I was hoping for a big hug and kiss on the lips from Moke's son.

In less than two days they managed to completely wire the house from slope-cans on the lanai to the water pump, to the ceiling fans and smoke detectors, to the sconces with dimmers in the bathrooms. They ran wires everywhere—inside the walls and under the second floor, drilling holes, going around pipes and even at one point drilling right through my propane gas supply to the upstairs stove.

In the first-ever gesture of responsibility on this house, Moke's adorable elf-like worker who looked like Dopey, the Disney character with his big ears and freckles, admitted his error with the drill and Moke paid for the patch. I was stunned that they didn't expect *me* to pay for it. I was also fascinated by the way he informed Moke's son of his error with a sober deference and humility you'd expect from a warrior. I expected he would have to lay down his drill before his master and commit hari-kari. He was practically in tears from the verbal humiliation he received after his confession. I felt so bad for him and tried to tell him it was no big deal, and who cares about a little gas line? He seemed to appreciate my kindness by asking me questions about my life in his melodic pidgin accent that I could barely understand. I was so grateful to finally be able to be soft with one of the workers who typically are painfully tough.

Moke's crew left a colossal mess—about two inches of debris on both floors. I had to call them to make a special trip down to clean it up before I would write them a check. I cut them no slack. Then came the big haggling session—seems we had a disagreement on the price. Moke's son and I went through item by item—they were charging me $60 extra for each additional outlet and fixture that I was adding that departed from the original blueprints. Grudgingly, I chalked it up to my ignorance and wrote a check for the extra amount.

Haole Monkey

After the electricians left, there was a comic moment to relieve the stress, though I certainly had not planned it as such. It happened on the eyebrow with the gutters people. The eyebrow, by the way, is that little roof that extends over an exterior door for rain protection. I think of Tammy Faye's giant tattooed eyebrows to remember what that thing is called. Anyway, like most everyone who has worked at my house, Aloha Gutters was called back to get the job done right the second time. I had called them back to fix a leak at the edge of the eyebrow. After they put silicone (think breast enlargement—see, it's easy) in the proper places, I hauled a bucket of water onto the eyebrow to test it.

One of the cute workers—a hapa-haole guy with only one hand—was down on the ground bracing the downspout to the siding when I decided to test for leaks. I let loose half of a five-gallon bucket of rainwater on the eyebrow and the water came gushing over the edge and down the back of the guy crouched on the ground. I heard the titters of the other worker who was standing back … that is until I unleashed the remainder of the bucket and a second gush of water got *him* down the front of his t-shirt. "Oh, brah," he uttered in wet anguish furrowing *his* eyebrows and surely thinking evil things about the haole with a bucket of water on the roof. I laughed like a crazy monkey crouched on the eyebrow and said, "Hey, now it's time for the wet t-shirt contest!" They did not find this amusing and returned to their truck in haste. They didn't even say goodbye.

They sped off with Israel Kamakawiwo'ole belting out a Hawaiian version of *Twinkle Twinkle Little Star* on the truck stereo. The leak was fixed, and at least *I* had a good laugh.

Chewy

Chewy is one of Mister Roger's beloved neighbors, if Mister Roger lived in a wacky white ghetto in the middle of the ocean with a bunch of fags, dykes, hippies, nudies, druggies, waste-cases, and general-purpose freaks. She came by the other day to help me paint. Chewy has a special technique that, well let's just say, cars would stop to watch her technique, were a car ever to go by.

Chewy gets her name from Chewbacca, the hairy beast of *Star-Wars,* lest you've forgotten. Chewy the dyke has a beard—not just a little fuzz, but a bona fide beard. However, she's no sideshow freak, and she doesn't drive a space ship. Chewy is one of my favorite neighbors who has taken to helping paint the house … topless. No bra either, brah! And it's fascinating to watch the male workers (that would be everyone else) trying *not* to notice Chewy painting with her boobs-a-go-go. They politely look at the ground when mentioning to her that the upstairs trim needs to be primered first. Actually, and strangely, not a single worker has asked me about her, nor have I caught a single worker stopping to sneak a look at her free-range hooters when she's not looking. They just ignore her partial nudity, or maybe it's just that by now they've seen it all. It is after all, Seaview, so why not a topless painter? Incidentally, one day I was driving by Kalani and a group of topless women were out front pulling weeds. It actually gave me great joy to see this brazen disregard for the law.

Van and Anne

Two weeks ago, I was deep in my drywall deliberations, torn between hiring one of two drunks—one in recovery who couldn't remember a damn thing and one well off the wagon who I hear starts drinking at 9 am in between snapping chalk lines on the gypsum boards. Each had given me estimates to drywall my entire house with a $3,000 spread between them.

Jay, the recovering alcoholic, bless his toothless soul, had pickled his brain so completely years ago that he mistook my job for someone else's and wrote the wrong date in the calendar. When he was ready to start before my plumbing had been done, he "quit" the job in a huff, blaming me. He had quit before he started. I simply couldn't believe the level of disconnect in his brain. Yo, Jay! Maybe taking up drinking again would be good for your business?

Enter the husband-wife team of Van and Anne. Van is a rather active drinker but a genius at sheetrock who can square off a corner so sharp it will cut you. Now, we all know that drywalling need not be confused with quantum physics or rocket science. So I say *genius* with a certain cynicism. But Van is good and he's fast. And he's twice the price of Jay, which put him about $3,000 out of my price range.

Terry and the Tarp Town Boys

Not sure of what to do about my drywall, one day I went speeding up Mapuana past Tarp Town—the collection of tarp tents that houses the five guys and two women building their own house a few blocks away from mine. It looks like the set of *M*A*S*H* with pornstars watching TV and tweaking their motorbikes. No less than 4/5 of the guys in Tarp Town are hot, young, motorbike jumpers eager to get work to pay for their biking habit.

Terry, one of the Tarp Town boys, called out to me and flagged me down as I was driving by, "Hey Dave!" I stopped and put the car in reverse. I backed into their driveway lined with about eight cars in various states of disrepair. Monkey Pod sniffed out the back window at them.

"Heard you were looking for a drywaller. How 'bout if we do your drywall for you? If we each pull down a thousand dollars, we're cool with that," Terry said.

"Consider yourselves hired." John, the quiet redhead from Alaska, and Bob, the tough blue-eyed skinny boy with black hair, stood by listening intently. Terry is the brains among the boys. He's also the oldest and the widest. As the alpha, it's his responsibility to parcel out the food. And so he landed the job for his dutiful and adorable co-horts. They all smiled and waved as I left.

The Tarp Town Boys arrived the next morning on foot with their tool belts yanking their pants down, exposing ample amounts of crack. They were a ragtag posse of biker punks carrying their boom box full of angry rap tunes like a war drum. Thus they set about the task of making my see-through frame of a house into one with walls, while I hurried ahead of them sprinkling boric acid inside the walls for roach control. I was thrilled to have finally found someone to do the work at a price I could afford, never mind the fact that they put greenboard (a moisture resistant drywall board that is typically used in wet areas) on the ceiling over the bar and in the bedroom, and covered a dozen outlets all over the house that I had to resurrect with the films I had made of the walls.

Bugs sizzled to their deaths in the halogen spotlight placed in the middle of the floor as they worked late into the night. I kept checking their work to make sure the insulation was tacked in properly, the right thicknesses were used for firewall, and the gypsum boards were not left out in the rain. But as far as the craft of their work, I guess I was simply unaware of just how bad it really was.

Van the drunkard came by with his wife and surveyed the boys' work on Sunday afternoon on his way to fishing and no doubt a little beer-battered cookout at the beach. He walked in, looked around and walked out in disgust but not before telling me that I was going to spend a lot of money fixing their mistakes. I laughed thinking I would spend no money on fixing anything—I would do it myself.

"No, really? What have they done?" I asked coyly, making mental notes. He belched out a list of what was wrong and that I should have hired *him.*

"Oh, Van, I hear you're good, and I would have hired you, but I just couldn't afford you." I stroked his ego by saying this. At least he'd get something of value for his critique.

"Yeah, I *am* expensive," he said with an air of arrogance.

"But worth it," his wife appended.

I smiled insolently without showing teeth. He gave me a list of fixes, which I've been working on for weeks now. I thanked Van for coming by. I was really glad he did, in fact, I was grateful—not that he had given me my first lessons in drywall. My gratitude to Van surely was not that I ended up hiring three guys who didn't know how to drywall. I was thrilled because I had made the right choice by not hiring an arrogant drunk. And further, the drywall boys and I learned how to hang, tape, and texture. And we're doing it together: three tough guys and one skinny fag putting up a house in the 'hood.

And so the schtetl is clearly under construction. Seaview has nearly a thousand lots—an oasis of development in a very rural setting, 35 miles from Hilo. And currently there are about 150 homes, a couple of roosters, several wild dogs, and a vicious blue and gold macaw. There's a town drunk or two … well, OK more than just two (and the way the drywall is going, there will be one more when this is done). There are even town criers screaming from the jungles.

Seaview will be a jammed neighborhood someday with its lots measuring just about one-fifth of an acre. It may very well devolve to the point where people will be fighting over their backyard fences with BMWs slipping in and out of electric garage doors. For now it has sweetness and acceptance—a playful sense of chaos that at the moment I find endearing.

There's nothing orderly about Seaview. It is a neighborhood without covenants and restrictions other than one must be moderately nuts to live here. Seaview residents are known to lose their sense of gravity quickly, and I can see how this much irreverence can get out of hand fast. I took a beer down to the water's edge and made a film about this lawlessness. Although I was illegally enjoying my alcohol in public, I had a foreboding sense that Seaview's lawlessness would come back and haunt me later on.

I'm a bit nervous and excited about Patrick's arrival next week. Since he doesn't have any work right now, I offered to fly him out to help finish the construction. I want him to like the house and be proud of my accomplishments so far. True to our dysfunction, I'm certain he will complain about it all and fixate on the faults immediately. Throughout each step of the building I've been thinking of him and wondering what he'd think of all this. His arrival is putting a lot of pressure on me to get the house in livable condition before he shows up. I found myself in tears a couple times rushing to Hilo to purchase more joint compound to finish the drywall and feeling like I've failed—the house is behind schedule and I've been increasingly tense. It is not in any way a livable house yet as I had promised him it would be. Patrick is arriving in the middle of this physical and emotional mess: something that is potentially going to be a disaster for him, for us.

In the meantime, I moved out of Don's jungalow and into my friend Chris' grand house in Puna Beach Palisades for a couple weeks before I move into the construction site. We nicknamed his oddball house "Heidi House" because it looks like a Hawaiian-Swiss chalet with its latticework and leaded glass windows that leak severely. (I stayed up all night once during a storm mopping up water that was coming in through the windows.) It offers some extraordinary luxuries that Don's house doesn't, like an electric fridge, potable water, and airflow to keep the mildew down. What a relief to not haul every bit of water from the county spigot six miles away, and to no longer be responsible for mowing the lawn—the house is set in the middle of a lava field. The deck facing the ocean is about a mile wide and the ocean view staggering. I was envious of Chris not having to build his house—no wonder he's always so cheerful.

Waiting for the whales and Patrick to arrive, I send my aloha,

Seaweed

17

Christmas, 2005

KALIKIMAKA TIME IN HAWAII

Day One Hundred Seventy-Three

Patrick arrived a couple weeks ago. Up to the moment he arrived at the airport, it was a mad dash to get the house in shape for his arrival. I spent two days in Hilo at Home Depot picking out toilets and sinks. I found it impossible to shop for fixtures without the knowledge of exactly what I should be buying. This has resulted in many trips to the returns line with my huge stack of receipts. At this point I have spent $128,000 and I have the receipts for each and every purchase. I'm savoring the frequent flyer miles I've accumulated for charging all the building materials to my credit card. I think I'll have enough miles for a trip to Asia when I'm done.

For toilets I ended up with the Eljer Patriot—an elongated toilet bowl—fitting commentary on America at this moment in history—a toilet named Patriot. Was I expected to salute before each flush? I'd be happy to think of George Bush every time I sit on the toilet. I especially enjoyed enlisting the help of a hunky Home

Depot sales agent to help me pick out an elongated bowl. I told him, "You know in the morning when you have that morning wood and you want to be able to pee—I need a seat that will accommodate that." A slight smile came over his face with a knowing nod. I must have either flustered him or annoyed him because he sent me home with bowls and tanks that didn't match. Another trip to returns.

Before retrieving Patrick from the airport, I nervously shopped several stores in Hilo looking for a lei for him, keeping an eye on my watch. Seems you can always find a lei when you don't want one. I ended up getting him a tuberose at the airport—a flower that is very strongly fragrant. I have a knack for buying things that Patrick doesn't like. It's almost like a disorder—I kind of knew it would be too fragrant for him and so I bought it. Then I waited in the open-air atrium of the airport for his arrival.

I saw his small and stocky frame coming along the exit ramp and down the escalator. I've always adored Patrick's creamy-smooth physical beauty—a light brown-eyed, black-haired mixture of French, Chinese, and Irish.

I choked on my breath so as not to burst into tears, and just put the lei over his head gave him a hug and did a pinched-lip smile. Breathless, I could hardly speak for a minute or two but managed to croak out a quick, "Welcome to Hawaii." He knew what was going on. Patrick never seems all that comfortable with my emotions—I think I remind him of his grandmother who always burst into tears whenever he came and went. There's something very vulnerable about Patrick. He's a bit like a lost child, and when you find him in the airport, it's like you've really *found* him at last—like you just found your brother that you lost in the ravages of war or something. And when you say goodbye to him, it's as if you're sending your kid to school for the first time.

This time I managed to keep it all together. He sniffed the lei and crinkled his nose. I could tell it was too fragrant for him and soon it would be mine. Perfect. All dysfunctions are Go. He commented on the new car as we loaded his backpack and suitcase, "A new car, a custom home in Hawaii. Uh huh." Basically he was commenting on how materialistic I've become. I took it with a grain of salt—Patrick would be (and has been) every bit as materialistic if he had the money to throw around. He loves to critique the very things in my life that he would do himself. It set the tone for his visit—he was not going to offer any warm congratulations on the progress of the construction. So I braced myself for the judgments to come.

We went for Japanese food at Miyo's in Hilo and caught up on all the gossip from Tucson including his story of seducing an 18-year-old virgin boy who works the front desk at the racquet club. He was now living in the townhouse in Arizona and still trying to figure out whether or not he liked Tucson. His ambivalence and paralysis sounded all too familiar, but the news of a sunny, dry, orderly place left me nostalgic for the Old Pueblo. I sat glowing across the table of the open-air restaurant, so happy to see his sweet and familiar face here in my new life where everything is so unfamiliar.

I drove him home with the glee that a father has bringing his newborn baby home from the hospital. I know this is a dangerous feeling to have with Patrick—it always results in an unhappy ending. I try not to go too high with him because the comedowns are painful and disappointing. Keep it cool, I told myself, he's not your boyfriend any more and he's not your baby.

We returned to Heidi House in the Palisades, and Monkey Pod came running out in a scramble of toenails on decking to meet Patrick. He wagged his tail so hard it made his head shake. Patrick likes big dogs and so we took him for a walk together under a crystalline panoply of stars. They seemed to like each other immediately. Patrick noticed by the way he ran with a little limp that Monkey's back paw was deformed.

I bought a few little gifts for Patrick including a sarong and some Tommy Hilfiger red sheets and a new foam mattress for him at the construction site. We had a few days at Heidi House before we had to move in to the chaos of the construction site. I put Patrick upstairs in the loft so that when he awoke, he could greet the day by throwing open a little glockenspiel-like door at the apex of the roof and have a jaw-dropping view of sunrise over the ocean.

In the morning we took Monkey Pod for a walk and had breakfast on the deck watching the sun sparkle on the Pacific. Patrick seemed eager to see the house construction where we would be living and working together for two months. So I drove him over. I wondered what this moment would be like for him as we turned the corner, to see the progress from the drawings on my computer in Tucson. The last time we turned that corner together, we were in Boner looking for a property to buy, when the lot was only a field of wild orchids. Now there was a colossal pile of debris, building materials, and something vaguely resembling a house emerging from a cocoon: the nascent beginnings of my Hawaiian dream house.

Patrick walked around the lot surveying it and immediately started cleaning, picking up nails, bits of debris, and cigarette butts to smoke. I tried to find where I scribbled his name for him on the eastern side of the slab in the direction where he was at the time. I guess the siding had covered it.

"Well, what do you think Sweets?" I asked him, but didn't wait for an answer. "Come a long way since you saw it on paper, huh?" I continued nervously fishing for some response, "You have no idea what I've been through. I've been working really hard to get it in shape for your arrival. Do you think you can live in it like it is? What do you think?"

Finally he answered, "Well, it's uh … well …" He nodded his head with tacit approval and a down turned smile. He was still surveying the workmanship and the messes spread out over the lot. I stood in the driveway with my arms folded in the place where we once stood together on bare lava debating whether or not to buy the lot.

I raised my voice a little to get his attention, "Do you like it? I mean, what do you think?" I asked again without waiting. Typical of my relating to Patrick—I didn't want to wait long enough to hear some criticism, so I changed the subject. I dropped my arms and headed toward the house, digging in my pockets for the keys to the French doors, "Well, we gotta get the cabinet boxes in the right places." And thus began our two months working together.

The first order of business with Patrick was a cabinet-making party at the construction site. Several neighbors and friends came over, ate pizza, and drank beer while John and Harlan led us through the assembly.

John helped me figure out the cabinet configurations and accompanied me to the warehouse to buy them last week. Home Depot was selling particleboard cabinetry that is notorious for swelling and falling apart in humid climates. I was in search of solid cabinets for a few thousand dollars—a tough order. Through some circuitous connections, I found a Chinese woman named Iris who ran a warehouse north of Hilo that distributed fruit, vegetables, and solid maple cabinets in standard sizes.

John and I arrived with a shopping list to find a massive open-air warehouse full of produce boxes with a petite woman in high heels in the back office: Iris. She greeted me with a thick accent and strong handshake before showing me the cabinets. They seemed of decent quality and they had one of everything I needed in stock at a price I could afford—this must have been a first for Hawaii. You

can easily spend about 10% of your entire house budget on cabinets. I handed her the list of what I needed and much to my surprise, she grabbed the key to her forklift, started it up and drove
around lifting boxes off the shelves and making a stack for me. It
was impressive to see a 5'3" woman of about 95 pounds driving a
forklift with incredible confidence, in high heels—shades of Pussy
Galore in *Goldfinger*.

On the day of the assembly party, we divided up the cabinets and
little groups assembled each one with screw guns attempting to
make sense of instructions poorly translated from Chinese to
English: "Please to thank you for your glonous purchase and ease of
assembly cabinet." [*Sic*] We managed without them.

Chewy, Don, and Patrick all worked topless. KiKi stood by
encouraging each of us and telling me how butch I looked wielding
a screw gun. Then we both ran off to pick up the pizzas from
Brie—the enterprising lesbian transplant from New York who
makes gourmet pizzas to order from her house down the road in
Opihikao. I was so grateful for the community effort and amazed at
how Patrick just dove right in, something he usually won't do. Folks
seemed genuinely glad to meet Patrick, hugging him on first meeting. He smiled graciously although sometimes I'm not sure he is all
that comfortable being hugged.

Later that week, Brie rescued Patrick and me from a fateful
nighttime lava walk. We set out on the afternoon of the full moon
to make the trek to see the lava flow. Patrick had never been and was
quite excited about it. It's about a two-hour walk, each way. We
planned it so that we would leave in daylight and have the light of
the moon to guide us on our way back to the parking lot. It was an
extraordinary view of the lava as the sun went down behind giant
waterfalls of orange magma flowing into the ocean with sulfurous
steam shooting into the air. Waves tumbled red-hot lava giving the

marvelous effect of orange waves. Patrick was amazed and thrilled to have made the journey, but we stayed too long, caught up in the excitement of the view.

On the return, we lost the moon to evening rain clouds and Patrick's night blindness slowed us down considerably. He was taking slow goose steps with me occasionally holding his arm in the pitch darkness as we traversed small mounds of pahoehoe. Without the moon, we lost our direction and began walking in circles. Then we saw a rock with a painted arrow on it—at last a clue. We figured it was pointing the way to the parking lot and so we set off in that direction. Unfortunately, it was the prank of someone who painted the arrow pointing at Kilauea crater. After about an hour we realized we were walking very slightly uphill, undoubtedly away from the parking lot.

Prudent people leave strobe beacons on poles at the parking lot, but I was overly-confident, having done this before. I would use the ocean and the moon as a guide.

It was 12:15 am when we finally conceded that we were hopelessly lost on a giant field of black lava, without a single landmark or clue as to where the parking lot was. We would have to camp out on the lava and wait until dawn. It wasn't a huge risk—it just meant an annoying night without water or food, trying to sleep on ground as soft as crushed glass.

All of a sudden we saw headlights about a mile away. Ahah, the parking lot! I flashed my headlamp at them and they flashed their headlights back to us. We were overjoyed that we wouldn't have to sleep on the lava and we set off in the direction of the lights. The kind people left their lights on for the 45 minutes it took us to make it to them. When we approached the car, it was Brie the pizza lady and her girlfriends come to have a late night smoke. She laughed her raspy laugh when she saw us, and we thanked her enormously for the beacon. The lesbians taking care of the lost gay boys—just like the AIDS crisis when lesbians volunteered at hospices to help the dying. It was nearly 2 am when Patrick and I returned to the house, exhausted and dehydrated.

Tonight was the first time that the house felt like safe haven—a comforting place to return to after a hard day—instead of the hard day being spent at the house and wishing in the evening that we had somewhere else to go.

Mele Mele

Christmas in Hawaii is an odd time. Driving along the rainy highways one can see flocked snowy windows, blow-up Santas in plastic sleighs, and lighted mechanical reindeer grazing on lava beneath palm trees. I find it a little strange that people who might never have seen snow, transform their houses into winter wonderlands. Those of us who fled those icicled lands usually have little interest in fake wintry Christmas decorations.

In Hawaiian, Christmas is called "Kalikimaka." Merry Christmas becomes Mele Kalikimaka in a loose transliteration. Remember Hawaii has only eight consonants and R, Y, C, S, T are not among them. All words must end in a vowel. So merry becomes "mele" and Christmas, if you work it out with a little creative letter replacement, becomes Kalikimaka. My name, for example, becomes "Kavika." Patrick and I, who really abhor Christmas, took great delight in going around wishing each other Mele Kalikimaka—it does sort of bounce, if not roll off the tongue. Happy New Year is "Me ka Hau'oli Makahiki Hou," which gives one a clue as to where Pee Wee Herman's character Jombi got the saying, "Meka leka hai, meka hiney-ho."

Patrick and I started Kalikimaka morning with a hike along the coast toward the lava flow. It was a balmy and blustery morning. White caps topped cobalt blue waves that revealed shades of light aquamarine as they thinned out, curled, and broke on the cliffs below. We mostly hiked in silence, enjoying the open space and appreciating being away from the construction site. Our hike took us along the rocky cliffs and out into the middle of vast tracts of black lava.

This time of year is hard on Patrick as both his mother and father died at Christmas. His father died on December 23, 1991, in the first year of our relationship. Being out in nature is comforting to him. We rested in the shade of a kipuka of ironwoods and I asked him how he was doing.

"Eh," he replied in his mousy voice, almost as if he were begging to be scooped up and held, though I know better than to try. History has proven that that would be more an expression of sorrow for him than it would be comforting to him. I felt his pain and kept my distance.

"Your father?" I asked, though I knew.

He nodded, expressionless. What could I say now that I had not said so many times before and that has been of no use to Patrick who sits there with a hole bored out of his heart from all his familial losses? We have so much history with each other that I usually know exactly what he's thinking and I know exactly what has failed conversationally, which I'm sad to say is mostly everything. We took a deep breath of salty air and sat in silent memory of his father who died a very painful death of AIDS in San Francisco 14 years ago. Then we headed home.

Feast of the Loons

Later on Kalikimaka Day, Jennifer, our neighbor to the back came by with her two-year-old son Tristan in a stroller and gave us a little bag of Kalikimaka cookies. I was very touched by this simple gesture, especially since I completely obliterated their ocean view with my two-story house. I opened up the sack and smiled at the handmade treats inside that looked as if Tristan had decorated them with sprinkles. Patrick snarfed them down before I even got one. There are moments of incredible generosity and kindness in Seaview that would leave me in tears—like the time when someone anonymously left Cornish game hens in the fridge for us. Then, each time I went away to Hilo to run errands, I would return to find another spiral wind ornament tacked to the downstairs lanai. It took a while to figure out who was leaving these gifts but the gesture of kindness was touching. It was feeling like the community had adopted me.

This is the lighter side of Seaview—a place whose dark underbelly remains mostly hidden in the jungles only to be seen on special occasions like Kalikimaka. The fine line between wacky and wacko is one that many residents of Seaview walk gingerly. And when they cross over the line to wacko, everyone in the neighborhood knows it. Today they cross the line.

On Kalikimaka, the open-air asylum converges at the big feast at the playground half way up the main road of Mapuana. The Seaview Homeowners' Association springs for a bunch of roasted turkeys, and the residents bring the side dishes. Basically, it's a big nutty family reunion with great food in the pavilion. Patrick and I decided to go since we had just moved into the house, and cooking was still quite a chore with makeshift stove and no running water.

We walked over and hovered about the edges of the gathering just in case we had to make a quick exit. I wore a black rayon sarong without underwear. It was so sheer that if I stood in the right position with the late afternoon sun behind me, I gave a complete silhouetted view of my genitals to anyone looking, it was like some naughty Indonesian shadow puppet show. I figured I would add my own brand of irreverence to the gathering, joining ranks with the Punatics. My lunacy was far exceeded.

The first thing I noticed about the gathering was the lack of familiar faces. Where did all these new neighbors come from? The answer I believe is that the announcement of free food in Puna brings people out of the jungles in droves. But where were all my buddies, John, Harlan, Bill, Mark, Kathryn? I spied Kimberly among the unshaved, toothless people talking to themselves with marijuana-ravaged voices. Patrick and I made our way over to Kimberly—always an oasis in the asylum. I clung to her for a safe haven of sanity.

This was our first Kalikimaka feast in Seaview, and Patrick, Kimberly, and I had the misfortune of being seated at a table with a guy who had just split up with his wife and was having a custody battle over their child. He used his hapless dinner guests as would-be therapists and burst into tears while shoveling forkfuls of vegan stuffing into his mouth. Honestly, I felt bad for the guy, but at the same time I had a glimpse of why his wife left.

Something was really off-center about this guy with his greasy Hitler-esque hairdo and deep insecurities, his devout religion, and his obsession with nutritional supplements for which he had handouts at the table. He stopped his diatribe about his wife only long enough to try to sell me some supplements and then returned to his story.

He's one of those people who inspire me to lock my doors at night in an otherwise, seemingly innocuous, albeit wacky place. His desperation seemed the subject one would bring up with therapists, close friends, and family, not people he had never met before. I felt hijacked—like when a homeless person comes up to me on the street and immediately launches into a narrative of his life without waiting for any sense of willingness to listen on my part. Patrick and I politely excused ourselves from the table and slipped out into the park and just kept going right on home. I looked back for an instant and it looked like the dining hall scene in *One Flew Over the Cuckoo's Nest*.

"Wow, Sweets, could you believe that?" I asked Patrick as we crossed the park, my sarong blowing up in the trade wind and showing my ass to the crowd.

"Toc-toc," he responded, tapping lightly on his temples as his French grandmother did to indicate someone who is "touched." We both laughed hoping no one would follow us to see where we lived.

Patrick and I spent the rest of Kalikimaka lounging about the filthy house, re-arranging the debris and tools. We were living amid utter chaos with dainty touches like candles and a tablecloth thrown over a plastic table that was cracked in the middle and had one broken leg. Patrick labored tirelessly to order the chaos. I just surrendered to it—this mess was nothing compared to the scene before his arrival.

Monkey Pod, Patrick and I were living downstairs where at least the walls were finished and painted. The dust level was now at a tolerable level. Upstairs I continued to tape, texture, and paint the drywall, occasionally discovering in the blueprints yet another buried outlet, hurling the attendant expletives at the cursed drywall boys of Tarp Town. The plan was to get the downstairs finished and rented to help make the payments on the construction loan and then move upstairs when the house was done.

We lived on used hotel mattresses (with cigarette burns) on the concrete floor with little rugs next to each one for wiping our feet of the powdery-white joint compound residue that was everywhere. Mosquito nets were strung over each of our beds. Monkey Pod slept on his green polar fleece blanket by the door. Mosquito nets and stacks of boxes containing fixtures and supplies gave us each some modicum of privacy, though I never quite got used to using the toilet without a bathroom door when the contractors were in the house. Once when I just couldn't wait for the workers to leave the house I covered myself with my sarong for privacy. It made me laugh—that if they couldn't see my face, then I didn't exist. Pay no attention to the man shitting under the sarong. We flushed the toilet with water hauled in buckets from the catchment tank.

There was a certain domestic beauty to it—other than the horrendous and constant disruptions of living at a building site—the simplicity of camping indoors with flashlights and hauling water was sweet. It felt like we were pioneers establishing camp in the middle of Wyoming circling the wagons around our piles of tools and debris.

On weekends, I puttered around the house fixing things and making bread in a bread machine I bought at a garage sale for $20. The house smelled oddly of paint and fresh baked bread. Patrick cooked, cleaned and organized the piles of tools and materials. He became known as "Abuelita" (little grandma), because he loves to keep things neat and tidy—sometimes too tidy. Monkey Pod's fur collecting in little black eddies was starting to bother Patrick—so one day rather than vacuuming the fur accumulations on the floor, I watched Abuelita take the shop vac directly to Monkey Pod and vacuum him. The noisy machine of course, terrified him. I thought it was pretty hilarious, but I'm not sure Monkey Pod was so trusting of Abuelita after that.

After a simple and tasty meal by candlelight, still with no running water, we would go out back to the hose attached to the water tank and wash the dishes on the lava. We called it the lava-platos, mixing Hawaiian and Spanish. When the dishwasher arrived from Sears, there on the box was emblazoned the Spanish word: *lavaplatos.* We both giggled. (This wasn't a coincidence—Patrick and I often amuse ourselves with word play.)

After doing the dishes under the stars, we would sit with Monkey Pod on the downstairs lanai and Patrick would smoke a discarded cigarette butt found on the property. He wouldn't consider himself a smoker if he weren't actually *buying* cigarettes. We admired the night sky and listened to see if we could hear the humpback whales singing as they surface for air. We were in bed shortly after dark each night and up at dawn working, cleaning, and re-arranging.

Breaking Free

Scott and Rowdie came for one day of work after Kalikimaka to install the countertops that I had painstakingly ordered from Home Depot who bungled the order selling me services that that Island Countertops didn't have. "Sorry, Mr. Gilmore ..." is always followed by some form of bad news and at least a half-day of panic trying to figure out a workaround.

In this case, Home Depot forgot to tell Island Countertops what kind of sink I had picked out, and they could not cut the sink holes without a template. Well, it turned out to be a good thing, because had they cut them, they would have misaligned with the supporting cabinets. *My* measurements would not have aligned the sink holes with the plumbing lines. With a cigarette tucked in a pinched corner of his mouth, Scott looked at the counters without sink holes and turned to blame me for picking them up like that.

"Why didn't you get the friggin' holes cut? We can do it but it sure is a friggin' pain in the ass—you should have had the friggin' counter people do it."

"Yeah, well, they didn't have the pattern because Home Depot didn't fax it to them. And it's a good thing, because they wouldn't have aligned. See?" I pointed out the misalignment under the sink cabinet. He blew out a puff of smoke in disgust.

Finally I stood up for myself and got a little hysterical. I told Scott I was sick and tired of contractors showing up when they damn well pleased and then while I'm paying them they stand there and point the finger at me when it's often some other contractor's fault for the mistake. My voice quavered and got a little high as I launched into one long run-on sentence, "I don't appreciate that you come out here and start blaming me when you promised to be here to do this job and I'm left to do something I don't know anything about and I screw it up and you're supposed to be here to help me figure these things out but I can't do it if you don't call me back or show up and it's putting me under a lot of strain …"

Rowdie pretended not to hear me, as he was busy screwing the upper cabinets to the wall. Scott just turned away from me while I was talking without ever acknowledging what I was saying. I guess he was referring my complaint to the customer service department in his brain where they put me on hold and eventually just disconnected the call. Without saying a word, Scott laid the sinks out, measured and marked the counters, cut the holes and installed them. It was very quiet that afternoon. I paid them for their time with the intuition that this might be their last visit.

Shortly after my little dramatic episode, Drainpipe Plumbing arrived to attach the sinks to the plumbing lines. For their final act, Scott and Rowdie had duct taped the backsplashes to the newly textured and painted walls while the construction adhesive was drying, and when we went to remove the tape, we also ripped off the paint. Just like my fifth grade art teacher Miss Almond use to say, "Mess up, fix up," *again.*

Like many of the contractors who came to the construction site to find me hysterical, lost to indolence, or just plain incompetent, Scott and Rowdie drove away that day in frustration. They never even said goodbye—and I never heard from them again. They wouldn't even take my phone calls and requests to return my blueprints. When I called on Scott's cell phone, I'd hear him pick up and then *click,* the phone would go silent. He was hanging up on me.

I found out later on the coconut wireless that Scott took a job working with a General Contractor making significantly more money. Small fry like me in this housing boom get thrown back to sea. They had promised to build and guide me through the construction from beginning to end. I think rather than ask for more money, they simply walked away from the job unfinished.

When it was clear they were not returning, I couldn't at first imagine going on without them. In spite of Scott's lack of forthright communication, they both had done an excellent framing job at a very reasonable price. The house was plumb, square, and level with very few mistakes. It was solid, secure, and safe and no one got hurt in the construction heretofore. Scott's building skills were top notch, and I think he will be happier working for a General. In my mind I wished him well.

Builders often forget what an emotional process house construction is for the owner, or they simply don't care. My working relationship with Scott and Rowdie had begun without ceremony and that's how it ended.

Now what in the hell am I going to do? Can I fly solo with the help of Patrick? I think this is where one turns to the neighbors who have been through this.

A hui ho, Seaweed

(That's "See you later" in Hawaiian.)

18

January 6, 2006

BARN RAISING, HAIR PULLING

Day One Hundred Eighty-Five

In the absence of Scott and Rowdie, the writing on the unpainted drywall was now quite legible: in this building boom if I want the house finished, I'm going to have to do it myself. Patrick and I have only ever done light carpentry work, so doing two bathrooms from beginning to end was a bit more than we had bargained for. We went on from there to doing drywall taping and texturing, pouring a concrete slab off the back of the house, installing handrails, hanging solid core doors throughout the entire house (and if you've ever hung a door, you know how tricky it is), roofing the eyebrow, etching and staining concrete, installing flooring, mirrored slider doors, pocket doors, trim, window sills, baseboards, appliances, and so on.

Little Patrick was an enormous help as were John and Harlan, the big girls down the road who came wielding an array of power tools. Harlan is a southern belle in his 60s who grew up in Oklahoma and owned a beauty parlor and artificial flower shop for many years in Tucson of all places, though we had never met until they walked by here one day. Years ago Harlan traded his clippers and apron for power tools and a tool belt. John, in his late 50s, is Harlan's amiable and handy partner who is dynamite with a sewing machine and a tile saw and a whiz at configuring cabinetry. Between the two of them, they had built several homes themselves. They seemed to know everything about building and jointly served as building oracles for Patrick and me.

They took an immediate liking to Patrick and converted back his moniker Abuelita to Little Grandmother, eventually shortening it to just Grandmother.

"How is Grandmother?" they would ask on their morning phone check-in.

"Oh she's fine, just hauling concrete for the slab," I'd answer.

"Shame on you—letting your grandmother do all the hard work. Well, listen hon, you're gonna need a big level and a screed. We'll be right up." And they would arrive to give us some direction, lend a hand, and provide some tools. They would call before going to town to see if there was anything we needed.

Throughout the weeks that they helped us, we had lots of laughs atop ladders and bent over saw horses, me working in my paint-stained boxers and slippahs, Harlan with his signature sweatband brandishing some sort of implement of destruction. John would get serious and take the lead. Patrick, Harlan, and I became his dutiful slaves. And probably for the first time in the whole building, I had some fun and got appreciation from those with the know-how. If I had hired *them* (though they were clearly not for hire), the construction would have been a joy.

John cut bathroom tile in 40 mph Kona winds that blew in from the west, when we had planned on the usual northeastern trade winds, which would have blown the tile spew safely into the driveway. Instead, the wind dispersed hydrated tile dust all over the exterior of the house and lanai. I was never able to get the stains off and instead had to paint the house one more time—this had to be the fifth time. Half of John's face was covered with the mess which made him look remarkably like the Phantom of the Opera on the side of his face that was downwind from the tile saw.

Harlan attacked the wall with his Saws-All to cut a window hole in the upstairs bathroom. Patrick grouted the stone floor in the shower stalls and cleaned up after us. I bought materials, textured the drywall, and did calculations of my burgeoning debt on the computer. And I painted, painted, painted. At times I had to stand on the lanai railing with one foot, hold onto the roof, and lean out to reach the corner hip of the roof with a paintbrush taped to a stick because I in my genius designed a roof with a four-foot overhang when most people only did three. (*Note to self:* A three feet overhang would have been sufficient to keep rain off the house and would have left most places within arm's reach.) Standing on the railing was a terribly dangerous thing to do and everyone who watched me winced with anticipation that I would fall to my death, though I found it strangely exhilarating.

We went on to do the concrete floors. Patrick spent days applying muriatic acid to etch and clean the slab. Then I achieved full-tilt insanity with the actual staining. At great expense I hired Scott Gebbe the concrete guru to come and stain the floors. It took him an hour and a half to completely mess them up, not putting down any protection for the walls, and leaving bare batches. Of course I had to pay him $500 and eventually had to repaint the walls. Many phone calls later and three days of neutralizing, re-etching, re-staining, re-neutralizing, mopping, spraying, and wet vacuuming—oh god it exhausts me just to write this—and finally we had a beautiful coffee-colored floor all ready for me to ruin with the sealer.

I went downstairs excited about doing the GemSeal and watching the slab's colors come out as it took on a glossy sheen. I opened the hugely expensive five-gallon bucket of godawful smelling sealer and began to roll it on. But before I could finish a single lap, the sealer had become tacky and was pulling the nap off the roller on the next lap. When I saw that I had ruined the floor with horrible lap lines and bits of roller nap all over the once beautiful floor, I went into crazed hysterics like Donizetti's opera character Lucia di Lammermoor. Patrick poked his head in to see what I was crying about. He stared at me. I stared at him with tears running down my face.

"Look what you're doing. You have to do it faster—you're ruining the floor," he said shaking his head in disappointment. He could see all our hard work being destroyed with the final step.

"I don't know how to do this. I *can't* go any faster or it makes bubbles. It dries before I finish one lap. It's ruined. I don't know what I'm doing building this house, Patrick! I just don't know," and I burst into one more loud spasm of tears. I wept holding myself up with the roller handle while he quietly walked away unable to watch me falling apart. It was probably the best thing to do—I was inconsolable.

It was such a disaster. I had envisioned a dark and smooth slab that would be so shiny you could skate in your socks on it when instead it looked like someone had laid out brown strips of paper across the floor with bits of exposed aggregate appearing right in the center of the room.

Another two days of phone calls and a second and third coat of sealer before I decided to *spray* it with a final coat to cover the lap lines with embedded roller bits. So I didn't end up with the smooth floor I wanted—it has a lizard-skin texture, which wasn't altogether unattractive. That floor alone aged me about five years. Interestingly, I lost ten pounds since I started building last summer, now weighing in at 125.

John, Harlan, Patrick, and I made the biggest messes known to man. But, out of the dust and horrible toxic waste I was starting to see a beautiful house.

The Tarp Town Boys and Birdman

Remember the drywall boys? Remember how I, in my naïve idealism thought I was going to have a transformative experience hanging drywall with the neighbor boys—the tough kids and the fag all working together? My imprudent drywaller selection turned out to be the single biggest mistake I have made. Terry, the alpha, came in and bossed skinny little Bob around until he was so frazzled that one day he fell off a ladder. Kevin, my neighbor who was building his own house across the street mentioned that he heard the crash and saw Bob pull himself up. Fortunately he was unhurt.

Then while Terry was having shouting matches with his girlfriend, Bob lost the trowels and the house keys in the backseat of the car while we all went crazy trying to find them on the site. Then they proceeded to bury innumerable outlets and switches behind the walls. They were basically begging to get fired. I had to actually go to Tarp Town one morning and rouse them out of their cots to get them to even show up.

Their texture work looked like someone invited an entire Waldorf School to throw tapioca pudding onto the walls and then smear it around with their fingers. The taping, what taping? And then how did the moisture-resistant greenboard end up in my bedroom? Perhaps they were thinking I might wet my bed sometime and would benefit from greenboard.

In the end, the greenboard by the bed was *not* a bad idea because the very first man I brought home *did* wet my bed. Brad and I met in the hot tub at Kalani—a handsome man about my age. We were kissing without doing much else. Certainly it was uncharacteristic of me not to reach below the water to grab his dick. He was a good kisser and so I just enjoyed that, inviting him over later.

He showed up, and we ended up in bed for my very first sexual encounter in the new house. When I reached down under the sheet for his dick, I found that there wasn't much there. My first instinct was that I had finally picked up a transgendered man. Given my numbers, I knew it would happen one day. He grabbed my hand gently and moved it to his chest and whispered, "I believe I owe you an explanation."

Brad confessed that he was born with a birth defect called hypospadia and that it required surgery to re-route his urethra away from his "micro-penis"—his words, not mine—to a valve inside his rectum. We worked around the issue—I always like to work with available materials, but then in the middle of the night he began spraying my bed with the rankest smelling urine as it passed through his rectum. (We cruelly called him "Birdman" in his absence because of his active cloaca.)

When he got out of bed in the morning, I breathed only through my mouth trying to avoid using my nose, and hauled all the bed linens outside for washing later. I tried to be polite, but smell for me is probably my strongest sense with men and if it's a bad smell, as in this case, I can never be with them again. So you can see how the greenboard by the bed came in handy.

In the end I just paid the drywall boys to get the hell out. I finished the job myself over the next three weeks re-doing the texture that they had so sloppily applied to the ceiling and calling them to come up and uncover all the smoke detectors and outlets they had buried. For hours I viewed films I had made of the walls before they were covered up, to try to locate where the electrical junction boxes had once been visible. One of the drywall boys jabbed through the walls to find them with a probe and then used a Rotozip to cut the drywall. Alas, uncovering them so aggressively with a Rotozip tore most of the insulation off the Romex and there was little insulated wire left for the electricians to work with. Moke would certainly unleash his ire on me for this. Perhaps I could get a spanking out of the deal?

Leaping Into Modernity

I had ordered all the appliances the day after Thanksgiving at Sears. I arrived a half-hour late after helping Kimberly pick out a new truck at the Mazda dealership and subsequently missed out on the post-Thanksgiving Day sale. I then stood around waiting for five hours to be helped. It's Hawaii, the computer systems are antiquated, and you simply can't rush people. I ordered two refrigerators (one for each floor), propane dryer, propane stove, dishwasher, garbage disposal and two microwaves. I managed to purchase a used dryer from a neighbor who was moving.

Exhausted from waiting and with my blood sugar so low I could barely drive, I left with a briefcase full of receipts, $3,057 poorer. The appliances would arrive in six weeks—the standard delivery time for anything in Hawaii coming from the mainland. And in six weeks they did arrive with the cutest guy yet delivering them with his very large and deaf assistant who was in danger coming up the stairs on the downside of the fridge. He kept pushing and couldn't hear his buddy yelling at him to stop. He pushed the fridge right over the top of the stairs, clipping the handrail until it landed with a window-rattling thud on the lanai.

There are times when I just have to excuse myself—things are beyond my control and it's best not to watch. This was one of those moments. I'll fix the handrail and sand out the scratches on the decking later.

Finally we had appliances, though still no fans, overhead lights or power outlets. Patrick and I ran the fridge, the one lamp and our laptops on extension cords running out the kitchen window to the temporary electric pole.

The plumbing in the house was working, and not by virtue of the goodness of Waterworks—the folks who installed the pump and filter, gluing all the valves shut. Moke generously came by one lucky day and gave us a 220 jumper for the pump so that we would have running water until they energize the whole house. Waterworks would not come out and prime the pump without an extra charge, so like a madman, I climbed to the top of the 10-foot water tank, filled the water intake pipe from a bucket and yelled for Patrick to flip the switch. The pump came on but was still sucking air. "OK turn it off, Patrick!"

I refilled the pipe and we repeated this routine unsuccessfully several times until Patrick walked away in disgust. I didn't give up and continued without him. I opened a hose valve so I would know when the pump was working. I ran back and forth from the top of the ladder to the pump carrying a bucket of water. And finally the pump sucked water, pressurized the tank within seconds, and water came gushing out of an open hose. It was as if I had struck oil. I was both deliriously happy to have figured it out myself and furious that Waterworks would not do it telling me, "I'm sure you can understand, Mr. Gilmore. It's a special trip for us to come down there, and you should have had the power supplied to the house *before* you had your pump installed, hon," Carmen whined to me over the phone. I have come to hate her condescending tone in the many calls I've made to her to work out the kinks of the water systems.

Whatever! My indolent self just hung up the phone. Now we have water, the single biggest step since the roof went on. The house's pipes pressurized, pinging and whooshing as they filled. The toilet tanks filled up without a single leak. And Patrick and I ceremoniously went to the downstairs Eljer Patriot toilet, saluted and gave it a good flush. Glory hallelujah, it worked! The house just went up a huge notch in livability from being electrified camping to almost suburban utility. No more hauling buckets of water. Contractors who have been peeing behind the catchment tank for months now have a real toilet. Sadly, no more lava-platos—I kind of liked washing dishes under the stars while Patrick searched for an after dinner cigarette butt to smoke.

With one more cord attached to the temporary electric pole, I was able to start the water circulating to the solar panel on the roof and within a few hours we had hot water. Patrick took the first hot shower while I filmed this glorious moment. Patrick seemed delighted to soap up and rinse off in the warmth.

After a few more weeks of working on the upstairs, finally it was ready to occupy, although the floor, doors, and trim were still unfinished. The final electric work had not been done, and the house was not yet energized but at least we could have a hot shower and a pee without running out to fetch water for a flush—what a miracle.

Patrick and I packed everything up and hauled it upstairs to the bare room with plywood floors stained with joint compound and primer. The living room has a very high 14-foot ceiling and a magnificent view of the entire neighborhood. Each time I arrive at the top of the stairs I stand there in amazement for having built this. All the effort seems worth it to live in such a lofty space.

Patrick set up the kitchen counter—a piece of plywood on sawhorses with a slab of granite I found at a yard sale as a cutting board. I set up my desk with phone and computer. That night I unpacked the DSL installation kit and in the simplest of procedures, the house leapt into the 21st century with high-speed Internet—such progress and so fast. The walls went up in just two days. The roof trusses went on in a few hours. Clearly, the biggest spurts of progress were the most expeditious ones, but the painting never seems to be finished.

With the Internet I no longer had to run to the Kalani café or Bill's house to get my email. Bill jokingly wondered if he would ever see me again. Now I could look up recipes, troubleshoot GemSeal, and check on serial commas for my blog all with my laptop at home. However, with the Internet, I lost Patrick to *his* laptop. Shell-shocked from all the chaos, he retreated into his computer, silently staring at his screen for hours. I understood and left him alone. I put on an Internet radio station from iTunes and for the first time we listened to classical piano music filling the house. It was sheer, unmitigated ecstasy for me. My beast was instantly tamed with the sounds of Brahms and Chopin. I just need about six more months of this tranquility and there's still so much more to be done.

Onward to the finish line,

Seaweed

19

Valentine's Day, 2006

LOVER, LONER, LOSER

Day Two Hundred Twenty-Four

Idealism is what precedes experience; cynicism is what follows.
—David T. Wolf

Well Dearies, it has been another very long stretch between journal entries of my new life in the middle of the big blue. I have taken inspiration from the occasion of Valentine's Day to reflect on a few things. First off, I want to point out that lover, loner, and loser are all just one consonant away. There you have it, my reflections on Valentine's Day.

Seaweed will now regale you with yet another story from the 19th Parallel within those rubrics. Prepare yourself for simulated exhilaration …

Lover

This is either going to be the short section or the bitter section. Being long-winded by nature, I'll choose bitter over brevity.

Today, just a heartbeat away from me as I sit here facing the butter-colored, hand-textured (did it myself, thank you very much) wall by my desk, legions of single homosexuals are gathered at Kalani for a summit of the flesh: the Hot Nude Yoga for Men and the Body Electric Big Island Retreat. Each year at this time the yogis converge here in lower Puna and prance around in the tropical sun lifting their knotted legs up overhead and revealing their naughty bits at the beach while the Body Electric folks are listening to top-40 opera highlights achieving greater heights of orgasm-less pleasure on massage tables. Meanwhile, I sit and look at my hand-textured walls.

And why, might you ask am I at home staring at the walls? The answer is simple. It is because I can. I have walls—four of them. In addition to walls, I also have the attendant PCSD (post construction stress disorder) leaving me not only unable to face the outside world of unpredictability, but financially ruined as well. I spent my entire savings and maxed out my home equity line of credit and had to start making interest payments on it at the new increased interest rates. Thus I find myself barely able to get out of the house, wanting to stay safely inside, sheltered from everything and everyone lest someone ask me anything about the house and I then stab them with a rusty trowel.

The last month or so since I wrote has been particularly difficult, perhaps *the* most difficult period of construction. I thought finding an electrician and drywallers was difficult; I thought putting the roof on the house in the middle of a tropical storm was bad. That was nothing.

When Patrick arrived in mid-December for two months I naïvely thought that the house would be just a few weeks from being finished and we would magically throw the switch and all systems would be Go. We'd soon be having drinks on the lanai and watching the storms pass over the meadows below.

After eight months of building nightmares, day in and day out—not knowing what the hell I'm doing, contractors who walk away without finishing and get paid way too much, inspectors who pick over things and tell me what I've done wrong, dropping boards on my feet, concrete hysteria and the likes, an eczema rash on my genitals due to exposure to toxic materials, I have deemed myself entirely unfit to love. That's right. Who could love someone who did *that* to his beautiful slab? Yes, I'm a mess this Valentine's Day and what I really need is a Hawaiian vacation (a vacation from Hawaii).

So, I'm sparing the folks reaching new erotic heights just a short walk away of my inability to be rational, playful, and sexual. Really, all I want to do now is scream and cry and maybe sit on the therapist's couch for about a year talking about construction war stories, applying hydrocortisone to my inflamed penis. It's not pretty, is it?

Loner

See above. Who wants to be around a maniacal owner-builder suffering from PCSD? Besides, I'm just reasonably pacified to be sitting here reading and writing while Monkey Pod goes around and around on his green blanket. I spend hours in the hammock rocking back and forth in the wind just daydreaming—my mind gone blank. Well, not completely blank. Seems all I can think of at this point are the horrors.

Loser

It's a lovely house, really. No, *really.* But I'm just too wasted to enjoy it. I spend my days counting my pennies, canceling my insurance policies, and plotting what I can sell to pay the bills. Maybe I could rent Monkey Pod out for someone in need of a little good cheer. Then when I thought I had reached bottom, the plumber called to tell me that they forgot to invoice me for $3,000 and that "the invoice really is just a courtesy and you should have paid us two months ago by contract." Somehow I missed that detail among the thousands of other details. Now they are demanding payment and I am out of money.

So who really is the loser? Is it Drainpipe Plumbing for developing a business practice that requires people to pay without an invoice? Or am I the loser for hiring them? Is it Waterworks who charged me $7/foot for 1-inch PVC pipe and then $362 an hour to install a water filtration system and then glued all the valves shut? Or am I the loser for hiring them? Is it Aloha Gutters for making the water downspout on the eyebrow lower than the catchment tank? Or am I the loser for not knowing this? Is it the builders who taped the backsplash to the latex paint that all came off when I removed the tape? Or am I the loser for hiring them? Is it the electrician who installed the house's power pole too far from the street so that the available cable *might* not reach when they do the swing-over? Or am I the loser for not telling them to leave extra slack in the lines? Is it my friends who laid flooring over a spacer so that there was a lump in the middle of the floor and when I stepped on the lump, it broke the plank's lips and created a crack that I get to look at every time I come in the front door? Or did *I* leave that spacer there? Am I a loser for standing on a ladder on top of scaffolding over the stairs to paint the lanai ceiling when the boards gave out and I slid down the planks and landed on my bony ass out on the cinder like a cartoon character? Is my builder a loser for telling me we'd be in the house in four months from the day they started and they'd be with me every step of the way, or am I the loser for believing him?

Isn't it romantic? Wouldn't *you* like to build your dream house in paradise?

The house did pass final inspection without a single hitch. It is at last, legitimate. Patrick and I did a little dance as the last of the inspectors drove off in his white Cherokee. I spent exactly $136,284 + property costs. But the house is still not finished. I have the eyebrow roof to do, more paint and trim to finish, the electric swing-over from the temporary pole to the power line and then the trouble shooting begins.

I'm sure someday I will find a sense of peace and will land back on my feet. I will forget how the framers, electricians, and the various Knights of Toyota tore up my life. You will have a lovely place to visit and vacation. And I will find a nice dye for my gray hair. I will regain some weight, I hope—I'm going on an all carbs diet as soon as I can afford to.

Aloha, Sweets

Just before Patrick left, Bill threw a farewell party for him. This is somewhat of an unusual occurrence—rarely does anyone ever get close enough to Patrick to offer a party for him. I think Patrick found this profoundly touching, and so he spent his last day in a mad rush looking to buy a piece of property of his own. He would get a home equity loan, much as I did, and start the process. It's still unclear if he did this solely as an investment or because he felt the warm embrace of the community.

I took Patrick to the airport on Friday and cried most of the way home. PCSD leaves me blubbering in the strangest places and at the most inconvenient times. If it isn't saying goodbye to Patrick, it's listening to Rufus while I'm driving. It wasn't that I was really sad to see him leave, tension had overtaken the sweet parts—a legacy of the epic David-Patrick affair. He was enormously helpful, though magnanimity was not his prime motive—I did pay him $15 an hour for his work and sent him the airplane ticket to come. I returned to the house stepping over his nickname "Dogwood" carved into the back slab we poured together. It was sweet to see him immortalized in the concrete.

Patrick was unable to find a property to his liking before his flight. But just after he left, a lot came on the market and he made an offer, which was accepted. He ended up with a piece of land similar to mine, two blocks north of my house—a parcel whose invasive trees I can see from my upstairs windows. Sight unseen, he became the sole new owner of a semi-wooded lot complete with junked Jeep. I sent him photos and video clips of his new land. Lather, rinse, repeat. Indeed.

As a parting gesture for the house, I had one last stroke of sub-genius to add to my list: A couple mornings ago, I was cutting trim boards for the interior doors and baseboards in a desperate attempt to finish the house entirely before leaving for Arizona for a break. I should have been using a compound miter saw, but of course I didn't have one and was at this point too broke to buy any more tools and too concerned that I had over-borrowed from my friends. So I held boards with my left hand and sawed boards with the circular saw in my right hand, bracing them on an unstable table. The very last board I was to saw was a short piece to fill a small gap—too small to lay on the table and cut with the saw angled inward to 45-degrees. So I held the board with my bare left hand, my index and middle fingers gripping it from the underside. I placed the saw blade on the line and pulled the trigger on the circular saw.

I immediately realized the stupidity of what I had just done. Yep, I had sawed through two fingers in a perfect 45-degree angle. My first instinct was one of self-condemnation—it was good to know that even in a crisis, my inner critic could still think clearly and deliver an incisive judgment. "You *idiot!*" were my words. The sensation of the cut was one that I have had a very hard time forgetting—it was an electrical buzz—much akin to sticking your fingers in an electric socket, while simultaneously feeling a steely slice, and then the vibration of the teeth of the serrated blade beating up my fingertips.

I dropped the board. Put down the saw and examined my fingers. I was immediately relieved to see that I had not sawed them off, though the cuts were deep. Blood was just beginning to work itself to the surface of the gashes. My body was trembling and yet my first impulse was to document it. I ran for my camera, hit the on button, switched it to macro, turned off the flash, and captured the flow of beautiful red blood pouring out of the wounds.

Ever since my high school years as the misfit yearbook photographer, I've managed to put the camera between painful stimuli and myself. I've always been the one behind the camera photographing the beautiful people—mitigating the sting of being unattractive and unpopular. Now I was using the camera to avoid my own physical pain. It wasn't until after I put the camera down that the sawed-off nerve endings began to throb. And finally I cried out. Monkey Pod got up from his blanket and seemed concerned. He smelled the blood on the floor.

I grabbed paper towels and applied pressure to stop the bleeding and ran downstairs to Ayako—the new tenant who had just moved in—to alert her that she might need to drive me to a doctor if the bleeding wouldn't stop. I also just wanted a witness like a wounded child holds off crying until it is with its mother. I kept my fingers tightly wrapped with paper and rubber bands on them and held them over my head to keep the blood pressure down. Miraculously the bleeding stopped after the second paper towel change. I had gotten off easy this time. With one hand in the air, I cleaned up the blood I had drizzled on the floor from the lanai to my desk, and in true Captain Ahab form, I finished cutting that damn board and nailing it in with the remaining eight fingers.

But I could not let go of the electrical buzzing and beating sensation of the saw blade on my flesh. It kept waking me out of sleep with a start to check my fingers and see if they were still there.

Today the ocean looks like an indigo backdrop as seen from beyond my computer screen. The solar hot water system is flowing with 160-degree water. Tomorrow the house will be energized by HELCO and the UV filter will make the rainwater drinkable. I am sorry Patrick won't be here for that momentous occasion that we both worked so hard for.

Thus the sharp field of lava became a slab. On the slab was built the frame. The frame became a giant, wet, jungle gym. The roof made the jungle gym into a dry shelter. The electric will finish it off—tying us in to modern American grid living, and I cannot wait to get the hell out of here.

I found a caretaker for the house and Monkey Pod, and booked my return flight to Tucson. Looking like a tanned holocaust victim, with my bandaged fingers as a badge of courage, yet too vanquished to feel any sense of accomplishment, I planned my escape.

Happy Valentine's Day.

Love, Seaweed

INTERMISSION

February 16, 2006 ✤ Bothered

Startled out of sleep by the voices
The blither, the blather, the endless chatter
I promise myself that tomorrow I will sleep in
Because tomorrow it will come
For sure

Walking at sunrise with Monkey Pod
I watch the moon disappear and
I'm certain that
If the wind would stop already, it would be just perfect
And if it gets here, then I can enjoy this more
And so I rush home—to check and see if it has arrived

Could arrive next week
When I'm finished with the painting
Or when the boys from nude yoga are here
Or when I'm back in Tucson
With my piano and my precious granite counter tops
And cool floors and hand-knotted rugs
And big screen TV

It has not arrived.

Well, how about a nap?
I switch on the air filter
The white noise smudges out the sharp edges
I squeeze in my dirty orange earplugs
And adjust the pillows
Turn off the phone
Open the window
Close the window
Cover my face
Uncover my face
Lie on my side
Clutch my pillow
Let go the pillow
It's too warm

Opening an eye, I scan the room for it
Trapezoids of light cross my floor
Then climb the walls
Monkey Pod watches me from his green blanket
Later it will be here, I'm certain
Maybe after I get my accounting in order

Maybe I should eat
I have that delicious red curry I made last night
I watch the fan twirling in my spoon
I should have toasted the nuts
Suddenly I remember my date tonight
YES, my date will bring it for sure

He announces his arrival
His old truck dragging the muffler
I run to greet him and throw my arms around him in the street

Our mouths meet after he looks both ways to see who's watching
I don't care because he has what I want
His wet lips touch mine
The texture of his tongue wraps around mine
Warm breath from his flared nostrils grazes my upper lip
He invites me inside to find his soft, slippery, warm center
We lie rocking next to each other brown and pink
Waiting for the arrival.

Clouds twist overhead
My roof opens up to welcome it
And finally it is here
I fill him with the proof
He holds me on top of him with his big paws and
There is no pain
All that was bitter is now sweet
All that was hard is now soft
All that was dark is now bathing in blinding light
And dammit, I forgot my sunglasses.

February 26, 2006 ❖ Dawn's Calling

Each morning I awake
Long before dawn
Is it the rooster that crows?
Or the painful realization
That at some point in midlife
It became impossible to hold me?

I grab my pillows and hide from the light
Ignoring that ungodly call before dawn
That reminds me to check
That empty place in my bed
And make sure no one is there
Still.

But today,
As the morning opened its sleepy eye
A faint light appeared on the horizon
And I knew something was different
It occurred to me here at midlife
That early in the morning
Still alone in my bed
Someone killed the rooster
And I can go back to sleep

20

March 10, 2006

❖

RETURN TO TUCSON

Day Two Hundred Twenty-Eight

Email from Don Falk: <<Welcome home sweetie. Don >>
<<Thanks, honey. Always trying to figure out just where that is,
really. Now I have two houses, and I'm not sure I have one
home.—David>>

I arrived back in Tucson on a Thursday morning after an overnight
flight from Honolulu to Los Angeles. It's a painfully long 17-hour
trip on American Airlines that takes me through five airports. To
help ease the tedium and smooth the transition from tropics to
desert, I treated myself to a double dip of Xanax in the Honolulu
airport. When I'm doing this, I make sure that I first get to the gate
with my boarding pass in hand so I don't space out, lose my ticket,
and miss my flight as I have done.

This time the double hit kicked in, my vision began melting, and
gravity seemed to overtake me. I could barely get off the chair before
my eyelids closed when they called my group to board. I did my best

Johnny Depp in *Fear and Loathing in Las Vegas* stumbling down the jetway like I had just taken a hit of acid.

I got on the plane and collapsed in the seat. Apparently the flight attendants had to sit me up and buckle me in. I have no recollection at all—which for me is the point of doing Xanax, of course. I awoke as we were coming in for a landing in Los Angeles with a giant wet spot on my light blue sweater and a nice viscous line of drool running from my lower lip to the center of the wet spot. I'm not an easily embarrassed person, but this time I turned a deep shade of red when I realized what a spectacle I had made of myself. I looked up and tried to laugh it off, wiped my lips and noticed that the entire University of Hawaii girls' volleyball team was on the flight looking at me and laughing. Later I passed the girls in the terminal and they snickered and pointed at me with my sweater still bearing a huge wet spot, "Look everyone it's the drooler!" Next time, only one dose or wear a dark sweater to conceal the drool.

Domestic Crisis

I keep trying to convince myself that home is on the inside, a metaphor for a place in my heart, not the granite counter tops and the glossy black piano. Such a simple concept, yet I can't seem to convince myself. I just love to cut veggies on a quarry of Indian stone and sing with my fingers tucked between the ebonies on a freshly-tuned grand piano. And so these beautiful (albeit bourgeois) indulgences give me pleasure and *home,* I argue with myself, is wherever there is beauty and pleasure. And so my mental pirouette brings me back home to my things. Rufus Wainwright wrote about this in his song *Pretty Things:*

> *Be a star and fall down somewhere next to me*
> *And make it past your color TV*
> *This time will pass and with it will me*

And all these pretty things
Don't say you don't notice them

My return to Tucson after many months of construction has left me in a deep state of confusion about *house* versus *home*. Somehow, the house in the desert—the one that I abandoned last year—feels more like a home this time around than what I was trying to create in Puna. Building the structure itself was not enough. Such a simple lesson learned so hard. I remind myself that there are no shortcuts to life's lessons.

Not being a wanton materialist, I have to admit that I'm at home cuddling with some fuzzy guy, or when I'm in the hammock with Monkey Pod, or even looking at the ocean on a sunny day in Hawaii. But I began to see how my home in Puna was also the home of the woman with the vicious dogs, the lunatic who accosted me in the farmer's market, the crazy bell-ringing screamer, the violent neighbor with all the restraining orders, the guy who wanted to kill me at the gas station because I wouldn't pull out of the way when he was done fueling. (I told him he needed to use the little gear on his truck—you know the one with the "R" on it.) In fact, there's a long list of people that I'd really rather not share a home with in Hawaii. It's not that Hawaii isn't considerably more beautiful than Arizona, but here in Tucson the mentally ill and dangerous are neatly tucked away or just lost in the mire. Hawaii's loons don't make for a cozy-warm feeling for me. They made me want to get a gun.

Patrick is still living in Tucson at the townhouse and he put together a welcome home piano party for me on Sunday. I'm curious how we'll get along. Patrick tends to be territorial about the house and is very set in his ways about things. My returning was like introducing another animal to a cat's den. It has to be done slowly with the first cat in a cage for safety. Without a cage big enough for Patrick, it was pretty much an emotional train wreck of a re-entry. By the night of the party we were already not speaking to each other.

Still, I was gloriously happy to be home. Even Patrick's cranky presence was at least familiar. I was overjoyed to be reunited with my piano. I sat and played a little Chopin, plucking out the notes softly—my fingers still sore from the saw cuts. The sunshine and the cheap food, the sanity, the organization, the trash pickup—all of it contributed to my feeling that I was more at home here than in Hawaii.

And yet at the opening night of the Gay and Lesbian Film Festival in this city of nearly a million people, only 150 aging, overweight homos showed up for the reception. It was kind of uninspiring. The pupus (can we call them that here?) were good, and the movie was bad.

I enjoyed seeing my friends and the flirty film festival staff member I once had bedded down. "Hey, you're back! How was Hawaii?" he said smiling in a leering sort of way.

"Well, it was wonderful and awful, and basically I think I like Arizona *better*—hard to believe, but it's true. The jury's still out." I found his lechery appealing—I was coming from nearly a year in a place where I was pretty low in the pecking order. In Hawaii, the queens who smoked pot, played volleyball, did the adventure tours, and were part of the inner-circle of Kalani snapped everyone up. I got sloppy seconds, thirds, or nothing at all. At least in Tucson there's no way I will ever meet or sleep with every sexy gay man in Tucson—much as I might try.

Oh, but what to make of Tucson—the town whose mediocrity I cursed a year ago? True to form, the Gay Film Festival is featuring a pretty bad movie, and it's sponsored by the MSN—the Men's Social Network (don't they know that's also Microsoft's acronym, and they're opening themselves to a colossal law suit?) that sponsors social events like pizza and pinochle night. Yawn. So I get in my old beater Honda—my Puna ride in Tucson—and drive home across the sprawl of dying cactus (130 days without rain, they say). Driving back through the desert I realize that I live in places that have both been ravaged by some natural and man-made disasters: lava and long-term drought, invasive species, and urban sprawl. Both are beautiful places, and both so fragile.

I slip in the house quietly clicking the front door behind me and turn off the courtyard light politely left on for me. With Patrick, it's important to pay attention to the small details like this gesture of welcome. I notice that Patrick has taken the bell off the front door—he hates bells. I cross through the house with the concrete floors done how I wanted them done in Hawaii—smooth and glossy. Opening the sliding glass door, I cross into the back courtyard with the baby cacti I planted a year ago now starting to thrive, toward the little brick house out back. The back house where I sleep and watch movies is my desert cave—a place that is endlessly delightful to me—120 square feet of pure beauty and pleasure.

It's cold out tonight—a real treat after a year of sweaty nights. I turn on the heat and the electric blanket to warm the bed. I sleep ten hours. No barking dogs—just the happy sound of the garbage truck at dawn. Across the Pacific ocean, my friends sit in their jungle house having dinner parties on an idyllic tropical island. I have to be the only person in the world who doesn't envy them.

I provisioned myself at Trader Joe's gleefully skipping through the aisles filling my cart with cheap, organic gourmet items. Goat cheese for $1.99! I was just beaming at all the culinary possibilities that even in my state of financial devastation from building the house, I could afford. I struck up conversations with friendly suburban folks who were shopping. The cute cashier was amiable and engaging—unlike the indifferent staff at Malama Market in Pahoa where you expect to get your change thrown at you. I guess I had forgotten how friendly Tucson was, its populace, no doubt, intoxicated by the endless sunshine.

One Week with Patrick

Saturday
Patrick and I met on a cool afternoon
Spied each other on the beach 15 years ago in San Francisco
In the shadow of the famous orange bridge
Like a big sister wanting her little gay brother to get a date
She bellows out to us a low wonk … then a high wonk
The fog has come in again

Sunday
Now we tear up the courtyard in the desert house
Pulling out the boxwood hedges and the bricks
I sift through the dirt separating rocks from soil
I shovel dirt into a red shopping basket and shake
My balls wiggle in my pants when I go side to side
My biceps flap when I go to and fro—
It's middle-aged gardening for someone with dog balls

In silence I sift
We don't really speak to each other
Not that we don't like speaking
Not that we don't have things to say
But after 15 years we know what the other is thinking
And we'd just rather not hear it.
Again.

I'm thinking, "Why the hell are you drinking my beer without asking

when you secret your wine away to your room as if I would drink
it?"
He's thinking, "Don't use my clippers that way, you're grinding
down the blade
cutting into the dirt like that."
I'm thinking, "Jeez is he going to tell me how much he paid for
those pruners again?"
He's thinking, "You ate my last two ounces of extra sharp
cheddar cheese"
I'm thinking, "You're a parsimonious little shit—I was cooking
your dinner"
And wondering why we're still living together

Monday
I put ginger snaps in his lunch bag
He goes to work to grade papers for $11 an hour
I stay at home and jack off and sit at the piano
Wondering what it would be like to compose a song like Rufus
My fingers still hurt from using the circular saw on them
I play the same chords over and over again
Hoping that maybe they'll sound better today than yesterday
Or that something will reveal itself between the black and white
spaces
I wait and wait and all I hear is train horns in the desert

Tuesday
We spend the day on line looking for dates
Patrick lies and says he's 34
I tell the truth
He gets the dates
I get the consequences

While he waits for his date to come
We dig out the old irrigation in the courtyard
We then move on to changing the grade
Now it's dinnertime.
His date never comes
Better to have lied and lost than to never have loved at all

Wednesday
My phone rings.
I have a date at last
I go to the back house and turn on the heater
I put on the electric blanket to warm the sheets
I get candles and matches together
I close the curtains and tuck a clean towel under the bed
I get the lube and moisturizer ready and some condoms
Just in case

I shave and clip my sideburns
Tame the wild hairs in my eyebrows
That are now like toothbrush bristles
I clip off the twigs growing from my ears
Smell my pits—just the right level of pheromone
Try on different underwear
I get hard seeing the white briefs
I never wear briefs except on dates

And then I wait and wait
Around about 10 pm I fall asleep watching the Antiques Road
Show
They're in New Orleans this week
I get up to pee and turn off the porch light and latch the front
gate

I hear the loud snoring upstairs and the TV still on
Patrick fell asleep with his mouth open
Somewhere between the Tiffany lamps and the 19th century
Maple Secretary
I guess his date didn't make it, either
I like watching him sleep
I wonder if he'll look like this dead
But a lot less noisy

Thursday
We argue about money and the extra sharp cheddar cheese
FINALLY! It's so good to get the cheese out of the way
And onto the next small token of our discontent

After dinner I crawl into my bed alone and watch a movie
It's about a small child abandoned
As an adult he murders in cold blood
His only friend betrays him
He hangs from a rope in the final scene
His body twitching

Later I hand Patrick the disc to watch
He is eating in his office chair
His feet don't touch the floor
He swivels to face me and fakes a smile
He forgot that he was still mad at me
Eating by the blue light of the TV
His ears are lit from behind by his lamp
Like red leaves stuck on a pumpkin
"Great film. Watch it." I say, "It's about you."
He doesn't. I knew he wouldn't
Now he remembers he's still mad at me

And he swivels silently back toward the TV

Friday
There's a note stuck to the door
In the tiniest of letters it says "happy equinox" with a smiley face
Those two words of sweetness
Scratched out on a 2x1 sticky pad attached to the door
It's all I will get
Does this mean, "I'm sorry I wouldn't share my cheese with you?"
I'm somewhere between touched and deeply sick of this
All I could write back is "U2"
It still hangs on the door weeks later

Working out on the floor getting ready for another date
I try to see what a man might see in me
Hair, not yet gone gray, swirls around my navel
It used to be a goody trail—now it's the welcome mat
I lift the 20-pound weights to tighten my flabby biceps
I lie down to do sit-ups on the floor
I notice an old picture on my wall of Patrick
Standing beneath that orange bridge of our youth
My stomach tightens
Maybe, I think … this will be good for my abs

The verdict I was expecting finally arrived: Patrick told me he couldn't live in Tucson any more. He wasn't finding suitable work, had almost no friends, and he hated the heat. He took a job grading papers for the "No Child Left Behind" standardized tests. After a few weeks, he left objecting to their politics. He then spent all his time watching television and reading by himself in his bedroom. It was painful for me to watch him languishing when I was so joyful to be home.

Patrick and I always put aside our resentments to say goodbye properly. I walked him out to his truck and hugged him once again trying not to burst into tears. It seems that I'm always parting company with Patrick on poignant terms. I ache for the sweeter times and yet when he leaves I'm always relieved to clear the air of tension, of my guilt that he's not doing so well. It's so hard to love someone who is so prickly and so depressive. I'm sure he'd say the same about me.

On April 27, Patrick returned to San Francisco to live with his other ex-boyfriend, a much more buoyant guy with a better wine collection. I hope it works out for him. I found a housemate to rent a room in the house here in Tucson and much to my delight he turned out to be a good friend.

The next morning I went out to the pool and hot tub in the piercing desert sun. The mesquite and palo verde trees were are all in bloom leaving puddles of yellow blossoms on the ground like a woman with a big yellow dress spread out around her as she sits in the middle of the desert. Hummingbirds were suckling at the giant orange flower stalks of the aloes. The days are warm and the nights crisp and cool.

I lay down on the pool deck with my arms outstretched hugging the hot pavement. My mind clicked back through the months, all of the characters who issued forth to help build the Hawaii house, the messes, the blood, the financial devastation, the endless rains, and then Patrick's latest departure. It seemed like my life had been on hold for a year, while I had a very strange dream with screaming frogs, blue chickens, erupting volcanoes, and a lost dog. I felt the warmth of the concrete on one side of my face and the comforting sun on the other side and I cried and cried.

Love, Tumbleweed

21

August 10, 2006

RETURN TO HAWAII:
SECOND IMPRESSIONS

The bird of paradise alights only upon the hand that does not grasp.
—John Berry

Have you ever noticed that no one *ever* says the words, "have to go" and "Hawaii" in the same sentence? I felt self-consciously pathetic about even saying them together in public, aware that I would receive absolutely no sympathy for my plight. People travel to Hawaii to get married. They'll bounce their grandchildren on their laps and regale them with stories of a once-in-a-lifetime trip to the exotic islands. They'll bring home plumeria-scented soaps, chocolate covered macadamia nuts (with hydrogenated palm oil) and flower leis probably imported from the Philippines. But me, I'm dreading the very sight of those islands—plain and simple.

I have had a complete turnaround romance with Tucson and the mainland. I spent the spring in Tucson and Santa Fe and then took a summer road trip to Santa Cruz, San Francisco, and Mendocino County with my wacky artist friend Max. Although penniless, I couldn't suppress my sheer joy at being back in Tucson, having piano parties, bicycling to a part-time design job, going to cafés and enjoying sinfully colorful sunsets in the Naked Canyon.

I was supposed to return to Hawaii in May, but I simply couldn't do it. The PCSD was still rearing its ugly head with nightmares of building inspectors and construction screw-ups. I postponed the return until August and spent the remainder of time in the Bay Area. I found someone to rent the house for a month and to take care of Monkey Pod, but the time away was coming to an end, and I had to get back to deal with my island life, my house, my car, my dog, and the greater question of staying or leaving for good.

And so I descend from a friend's hilltop apartment in San Francisco with two rolling suitcases pulling me kicking and screaming toward the subway station. I just want to point out, that managing two rolling suitcases in San Francisco on a third degree down-slope is just about more fun than a 42 year old should have. I practically had to put my arms back in socket and discard my torn up shoes by the time I got to the bottom of Douglass Street in the Castro.

And so onward I went with my own version of the Trail of Tears—banished to the Big Island for late summer: rain, bugs, crazy people, and rotting fruit everywhere. I could hardly wait. The highlight I thought will be my chance to take Xanax and space out in the airport, perhaps even drool all over myself again on the flight crossing the Pacific.

There are times when life is simply too raw for me, and so I just take a tranquilizer and check out. Anyone who knows me is aware that I regularly face my fears head on. But leaving San Francisco is just one event that I would rather erase with Mommy's Little Helpers. Patrick remembers the time he drove me to the airport in San Francisco a few years ago—shortly after I had first moved away to Arizona. The waterworks started just about the time he turned the key in the ignition, and I couldn't gain control. I sobbed all the way to the airport. That time I was flying back to Tucson. Ironically, that's exactly where I'd rather be going now than the most remote island on earth.

So what gives? Remember a year ago how excited I was to be leaving Tucson and starting a new life in Hawaii? I shipped my most precious items (except for the piano) in boxes, bought a car, and began laying foundations for a new life there. So what happened? Well, if you've read my previous journal entries you know that I have become terminally disenchanted with this enchanting place during the course of a year. In that year, I crossed over the threshold that tourists never do and that I had never done in the months I had spent vacationing in Hawaii.

As a tourist you have a protective skin of vacationer-glow that keeps you from noticing the dark side of a place, unless of course it hits you over the head like a falling palm frond. The tourists who have been pulled out of their convertibles in Kapoho and beaten up simply for being tourists certainly have gotten an up-close and personal view of Hawaii's underbelly. How can a land be so beautiful at one once and yet so dark? To answer this question, you'd have to read up on your Hawaiian history. If you've never taken an interest, here is my one-minute overview:

> Europeans stumbled upon Hawaii in 1778 bearing the unwelcome gift of smallpox while at the same time introducing European invasive plants and animals that killed, ate, and overtook virtually every living thing on these lovely islands. The missionaries followed suit and infected the remaining people with their pernicious religion.
>
> Then the Hawaiian royalty said, "Hey we want some of those foofy clothes and architecture, so let's go to Europe and give our royal families some bling and pimp our royal cribs." While they were off partying in Europe at Queen Victoria's jubilee, the American industrialists appointed to cabinet positions before they left, took over the Hawaiian government and

deposed the monarchy. Surprise, surprise, surprise.

The American industrialists, sought out by the royal family for investment in the islands, brought over workers for the fields from Asia and the Philippines. The US government smelled the opportunity (sound familiar?) and tightened the choke collar protecting their economic interests and the future of a mid-Pacific naval base.

Today Hawaii is one of the poorest and least-educated states in the nation. It is the ugly result of imperialism, exploitation, and neglect. In short, it's Alabama with volcanoes.

So there it is: a brief history of Hawaii and the genesis of its underbelly. Can we blame the locals for being angry? Not really. But does their entitlement to redress justify personal retaliation? Is it right to yank those ghost-like tourists with the funny hats out of their cars and beat the sunscreen off them?

Drugs, poverty, lack of education, and loss of native homelands have caused this place to go agro and unfortunately my friends and I unwittingly shoulder the burden of trespasses wrought long ago. Most people I know would like to make a difference but what can we do? I don't have the political power to have any impact other than leading my own life with integrity. Speaking up, learning a little bit about Hawaii and its history and culture is helpful and may very well be all I can do.

But when you have the drugged-out Hawaiian guy in the house across the street junking his cars in the field and letting his dogs bark all night long and yelling at haoles to go home, I think, "Well, you're not really going to win much support that way." And is that really respecting the "aina" (land)? The world is an unfair place. There are injustices everywhere. Presumed privilege isn't always a gift and you know, the Hawaiians were really not a very peace-loving people to begin with.

The Native Hawaiians, as we think of them today, came from Tahiti to these islands already inhabited by the Menehune. Legend goes that the Menehune were small people and the Tahitians rather large. So they overtook the Menehune and in effect stole their land. Fourteen hundred years later, the bloodthirsty King Kamehameha (dubbed "Hawaii's Greatest King" like Ronald Reagan was the "Great Communicator") united the islands by killing off anyone who stood in his way. Hawaii has always been ruled by a violent or oppressive and opportunistic oligarchy and now as an occupied nation, at least there is the chance for due process of law and everyone to own property and to become piggy capitalists. "Shoots, brah!" (That's *cool, dude* in pidgin.) All of this history has made for an angry vibe about the place. Combined with the isolation and the loony-tunes wandering the open-air asylum, I'm not sure I can bear to live in Hawaii any more. I'm waiting for a sign to convince me one way or the other.

I get to the airport in Oakland after an attempt was made to swindle me into buying a bogus ticket for the shuttle, and I find several friends on the same non-stop ATA flight to Hilo. This is a good sign, I think. The Dandelion Dance Company is on the same flight, and when the plane is delayed an hour, they break out the violin and start dancing.

Wailana, a dancer I have seen at Kalani and at Kehena Beach, takes one of my Xanax, spaces out on the flight and just walks away in Hilo without saying thank you, aloha, or goodbye (and of course he never even asked me a single question in the two hours we sat together in the Oakland airport). I guess being pretty means never having to take an interest in anyone else. Cute boys lacking social graces—I guess I can't really pin that on Hawaii. It is a bad character trait that is somewhat universal.

So now I'm back in the hammock here in Puna. Two nights ago, the moon was approaching being full, which I suppose could explain the bloom in neighborhood hostility. My neighbor Harry was screaming at full volume into the jungle for hours before I went down to see if he was OK. He came out of his jungalow, cried and told me that after 14 years of his yelling in the jungle, no one has ever come to check on him. He's kind of like that friendly monster in *Rudolph the Red-Nosed Reindeer* who just needed some dental work to tame his inner beast. Harry wanted someone to listen to him, but yelling for a decade and a half has not done any more than inspire his neighbors to put in earplugs. Maybe a new strategy is needed.

Two cats shrieking like teething babies took to slicing each other up at about 3 am, and then at dawn the lady down the street took off with her son chasing and yelling after her car. A screaming match with his sister ensued back at the house, and then two gunshots were fired. If I smell bodies rotting, I'm calling the police, but not a moment before. (I confess, I am hoping for a double homicide.) At about 11 am, Terry and his girlfriend launched into one of their famous rows at Tarp Town. I lost my cool, cupped my hands to my mouth and yelled back, "Can I get you some sharp objects?"

Kimberly, who lives just a couple blocks "mauka" (uphill) from me, has an odd affection for the local Punatics. Somehow she's not rattled by the hostility on parade. I, however, am ready to call Hezbollah to see if I can order a rocket launcher. So you can see how Tucson with its covenants, codes, and restrictions suddenly seems appealing. The mundane middle class of a mid-sized city is just soothing balm to someone tortured by the blowhard jungle trash that abounds here living without much needed anti-psychotics, teetering dangerously on the edge of reality.

Now Who's Nuts?

Last night, Kimberly and I went to a "full-moon psychedelic erotic café" party at Kalani. I planned my outfit to include a pink butt-plug with rubber pigtail protruding from my ass. I wore that and a pink cowboy hat and nothing else. Kimberly agreed to help me into my outfit—rather my outfit into *me*—as long as whatever she did would still leave her lesbianism intact. I promised. She got a couple pictures of me bending over the bumper of my car and exhaling, trying to get the pigtail inserted.

Just before we reached the front door of the party, my plug dropped out onto the cinder. Dang. My outfit malfunction was creating a scene while picking up sharp bits of cinder, which would do no good for my rectum. I waltzed over naked to the hose, rinsed my outfit off, bent over and reinserted it with a groan and walked into the party. I found it a little difficult to hold it in without tensing my entire body. Relaxed conversation would be nearly impossible looking like I was about to have a big shit.

Of course, this is Kalani, a time-warped extension of San Francisco in the 70s. No one notices anyone over 30, butt plug not withstanding. In Tucson, I would be banished from the social scene forever, but at least I would have been noticed.

I let the butt plug plop out onto the dance floor for the last time and unceremoniously tucked it away in my backpack and opted for day-glo body paints instead. A lovely woman named Cheryl painted my balls neon blue while I explained to her the meaning of the metaphor. As a lesbian, she never had the joy of being a sexually unfulfilled teenage boy with blue balls. Thank the goddess for that.

Kimberly and I spent the evening trying to dodge mushroom conversations when really all I wanted to talk about was the Fed chairman's latest edict about the economy and Joseph Lieberman's defeat in Connecticut. I watched a guy named David engage in a petting ballet with the beautiful (and half his age) Hector from the

Dandelion Dance group. Hector rolled over, face down onto David's lap while David massaged his smooth back and held his perky butt. Being that they were tripping, I'm sure they sensed my envy on a cosmic level. I wondered what I looked like to them—maybe some sort of hairy stick insect—a praying mantis?

I stepped outside for a moment and thought about how queer it was that in this remote jungle we freaks should all be standing around painted in day-glo colors throwing an erotic, psychedelic party. I have to admit there are some intriguing things about Hawaii, its history and its people. Maybe choosing between two places or lashing one's identity to only one place is pointless.

Hawaii's stunning beauty hits you like a crashing wave—taking you on a white water tumble. Then it holds you in its wet arms as you swim away from its perilous shores, if you are strong enough to make it beyond the breakers. Its abundant rain showers wash you of your identity and leave you raw as a bleeding volcano.

Arizona's stark and subtler beauty is found in the blinding still-ness of the desert sky and the Zen-like simplicity of the desert. You must take the time to spelunk its charms in caves and canyons, its derelict downtowns whispering to you late at night with a lonely train horn. It comforts you in the shade of a lush Mexican courtyard or within the thick walls of an adobe house.

Standing outside the screened shack at the party, on the edge of a jungle so thick it just might grab you if you get too close, I won-dered what the spirits of the Menahune would think peering at us in our psychedelic party.

Perhaps they'd be wondering if we had high-speed wireless so they could find the nearest shoe store. Still waiting for a sign …

Aloha for now, Seaweed

22

August 30, 2006

QUAN YIN AND THE PARTY BOYS OF LOWER PUNA

I used to want to change the world.
Now I just want to leave the room with a little dignity.
—Justin Bond from the film *Shortbus*

Sometimes I think that I live for nothing more than to tell a story. That I should even set out for an evening's event with the hopes of getting some tasty morsels of material for my blog, has called into question my own appetite for real experience.

The following story is what emotional paramedics might call a "bleeder." If you're one of those people who prefers to couch everyone's pain as a choice, or the description thereof as whining, then I invite you to skip to the next chapter. I'll be here carving my neuropathways with a steely knife listening to Rufus.

One little note for the ultra-compassionate among you—I'm fine. Really. Writing is sweetener for the often very bitter taste of life. You don't need to send someone over to check on me, though if you brought me a lasagna, I wouldn't mind. My hope is that perhaps you'll read this and either relate to it or just let it wash over you like the words of a song you don't understand but you listen to it anyway because you know there's something ineffably appealing about it.

You've heard me drone on before about how I don't fit in here in the queer jungles of Hawaii. Something about me is hell-bent on trying to resolve my issue of being a misfit. Or is being here just further salting my wounds? I guess I'm confused. If I sat home and ignored a party that was going on, mind you a party I wasn't even invited to, I'd feel like I'd missed an opportunity for something—to meet friends, have a good time … *something*. But then again, if I were to go to one of those parties uninvited, the tone is already set that I don't quite have a sense of belonging at that gathering.

In a way I'm like Patrick's little French and Chinese grandparents. I visited them in the bleak town of Oroville, California for Christmas in 1995. In their 80s they didn't receive too many invitations but when they did, they dressed up, shaved, and perfumed their delicate old bodies and would sit beside each other on the sofa with coats on, silently listening to the antique clocks ticking away the seconds until the time of departure. I, like Patrick's grandparents take party invitations seriously. I shave, work up an outfit, and think about whom I might encounter and try to show some interest in their lives.

Patrick carried on his grandparents' tradition, and in his 30s in San Francisco, he didn't receive too many invitations. He's a bit of a recluse, but when someone did invite him, he'd arrive punctually and dressed for the occasion. One lavish Christmas party at a friend's in San Francisco, he arrived wearing an ill-fitting, second-hand suit and his grandfather's navy wool overcoat—an ensemble to break your heart. You could tell this was a man who was more comfortable in worn-out hiking shoes, covered with dirt and compost, digging away in his garden.

So Patrick's effort to dress for the occasion, albeit not terribly well executed, was honorable. I remember actually having to hide behind a sumptuous yuletide buffet to cry—he looked just like his tiny Chinese grandfather, nervously trying to muster a smile and clenching his little hands under the too-long sleeves, hoping that someone would notice his arrival. I did, hoping no one would notice *me* sobbing at the buffet table.

It's interesting to see how as an adult, my childhood wounds of being unpopular get fleshed out in my modern-day, jungle version of high school. Driving by a house in my neighborhood with cars lining the road is an immediate trigger: why am I not in there with them? Should I just go in anyway? I do have some sense of propriety about these things and if not extended an invite, I don't go. But a stone out of water doesn't get polished and so sometimes I do just show up and work through my issues of exclusion.

The last party I attended, I arrived naked with a pigtail buttplug popping out of my ass—dressed for the theme of a psychedelic erotic café. Last night's party was in celebration of David Sanders' 53rd birthday—a flip-flops and shorts affair. David is a very well-preserved and toned yogi and spiritual seeker living in a mid-century trapezoidal house that looks a bit like Pee Wee Herman's playhouse with its slanted walls and candy colors.

I arrived once again with Kimberly (figuring at least if I'm not invited, I might as well arrive with someone so I don't look like a total loser), this time also accompanied by her brilliant 16-year-old son, Caleb. Party going with Kimberly is always a joy because Kimberly has unparalleled social skills. As a self-identified "femme" lesbian, Kimberly is a master at the art of putting people at ease conversationally and with her delicate and intentional touch. Moreover, Kimberly is an entire buffer zone between myself and the many socially inept gay men that inhabit lower Puna. She sits like Quan Yin (albeit, with a nicer rack) at the edge of the dance floor pouring out mercy and compassion for all us homos prancing around dodging glances in dark sunglasses and revealing just enough butt crack and bicep to taunt each other into an ecstatic state of disconnection.

I stood on the front lanai greeting various people as they came up the steps toward the rush of loud dance music. I figured I might as well give myself a purpose and be the greeter. Tonight, typical of my experience of Puna, half a dozen or so beautiful men walk up, see me and give me a half-smile and while I'm saying hello, quickly look away to see whom else might be nearby. It's a scenario that has repeated itself so many times that if I had a dollar for every time it happened, I could buy mufflers for every car in Seaview. Honestly, though, the sting of it has never stopped.

I walked inside to greet the host and birthday boy. I had rehearsed how I would explain my appearance at a party to which I was not invited. In my hug of the host, I said into his ear, "Hi David, I wasn't invited, but I came anyway. And happy birthday." His response was not one of shocked disbelief that I often encounter here when hammering people with some truth that they'd rather not hear.

Instead he said, "You are *so* invited." I smiled and felt slightly sheepish about foisting my angst upon him. He had said, after all, the perfect thing.

As the light faded and the mosquitoes hovered about our ankle buffets, the music got louder, the trade winds stopped, the temperature went up and the shirts came off on the dance floor. Men revealed their moist and lithe bodies, wisps of hair curling around their nipples and navels as they each danced solo.

The seriously inked-up Aka was earnestly controlling the music from his laptop, bent over the console with a little underwear and tattoo showing on the small of his back. Three Raven was waxing about how the body out of balance breaks and Mojo was complaining about his enlarged pores.

At parties, I always notice the people who don't fit in—the ones who sit on the side or stand by themselves, clutching a beer bottle for security. Often I will talk to them but usually they can tell that I pity them and by this time they have become feral. Honestly, I'm hoping that someone notices that I'm often that one with only the beer bottle for company. And so I pray for Quan Yin to rescue me and she does. "Did you see how that guy just walked away while I was talking to him?" I say to her.

Kimberly, in her infinite ability to say what's so in the most palatable way possible replied, "You see, David Darling," (she always calls me David Darling to soften the blow of some horrid truth I need to face), "they're dealing with the same insecurity you are. They're looking for someone to validate them."

With a little kick from Kimberly, it occurs to me that perhaps we're all in this together. And maybe if I took psychedelics like a normal person I would have a greater understanding of this unspoken commonality. Kimberly has been mistaken for someone who does drugs to help her achieve her bliss. She doesn't, but maybe I ought to.

One bright light of conversation was with a beautiful young man whose name I'm going to leave out because the details of this are going to be such that he'd probably prefer I didn't reveal his identity. I had met this man before and appreciated his youthful earnestness and social skill. He came to the table where I was blotting my greasy forehead after a pirouette through the steamy dance floor. He offered to get all of us some cake. I knew these were manners cut on the mainland East Coast. People from the West Coast have an attitude of, "I trust that you know how to take care of yourself and ask for what you want, and so getting your own cake really is your way of empowering yourself." Someone from the northeast would say, "Anyone want cake?" And he went to fetch cake for those of us who nodded.

I also noticed this man was straight. Oh goody, goody, I thought, I just love straight men. In a land of pleasure-obsessed gay men, straight guys can provide all the camaraderie I want and engage in conversation without the fear of having to dodge a sexual advance. It just usually doesn't occur to straight guys that other men might be flirting with them and so they aren't self-conscious and aloof. If a hand is thrown out for a firm handshake and a strong, "Hi, I'm Jeff," you can usually bet that Jeff is going to be straight. If a man slinks into a room and skirts round the edges, silently checks out the scene (and people's footwear), locates the exits first, and then stands there ignoring everyone hoping that the cutest person in the room (whom he has already picked out) will come over and introduce himself, then you can pretty much bet this is a gay man. Ironically, the cutest man and the only man with the confidence to introduce himself will almost always be straight.

"This Man," as I will call him, (the one fetching cake), began to express an interest in "This Woman," another friend of mine whose name I will also leave out. I never imagined that within two hours, I would be holding the hairy nuts of This Man while This Woman gave him a blowjob.

As a gay man, it's pure entertainment to watch a man flirting with a woman—a lion scoping out his next conquest from atop a hill. There's no rejection in the equation for me because I know there's no chance of an erotic exchange, and so I enjoy by osmosis the hunt, the smell of a man in heat. I get to watch him trying to balance cool and caring as he approaches the object of his conquest.

What was unusual about this flirty interchange was that This Woman was my age and This Man was 17 years younger. Women, you know, always hold the sexual trump card but in this case This Woman had the royal flush and the sexiness and power to play that hand until This Man surrendered. This is where the storyteller in me took over the helm. I was fairly certain nothing erotic would come my way this evening with This Man and This Woman, but I could certainly watch and help orchestrate it for the story. I pulled out my mental notepad and began scribbling notes.

Now, what a gay man has over a straight man is easy access to women's hearts. We can sit in the colorful stinging tentacles of a prickly woman like a Clownfish sits un-stung in a sea anemone waiting for morsels of meat that are left over. Gay men have a pro-tective coating that allows us to be soft and easy and trusted with women. On the contrary, a straight man is regarded with extreme caution—he must earn a woman's trust. This pressure can bring out the worst in the man—a nervousness that results in the man talking too much, boasting, drinking excessively, and tossing money about carelessly.

Another interesting contrast—a learned behavior—is that straight men must go slower than gay men with the objects of their desire if they are to score. A straight guy can go *so* slowly that he can lose the momentum to endless processing and niceties culminating with just a kiss on the doorstep and end up home alone with his dick in his hands. A gay man rarely ever passes up an opportunity to go all the way, and it's a pretty fast track to the bedroom.

Gay men go so fast that they can be off to the bathroom having sex and make it back to the dance floor before the next Gloria Gaynor song has finished. Here is where this envoy of gay culture was going to have to intercede. If I was going to get a juicy story, and these two were going to get it on, I was going to have to assist and step on their gas pedal a bit.

I made sure the two had met and then soon after complaining about the heat, I said, "How about a night swim at Kalani?" They both seemed relieved that someone suggested an event that would both relieve us of our clothes and cool our sweaty bodies. I was relieved to be bailing on a party that was making me hate everything about gay men.

We arrived at Kalani and spent an hour floating naked in the pool and hot tub under a beautiful view of the open arms of the Milky Way galaxy. This Man took off to the shower for a moment and left This Woman alone with me. Floating on noodles in the pool, we quickly strategized in hushed tones and giggles about what we wanted tonight and how we were going to achieve it. This Woman is really a gay man in a woman's body and so we were instantly aligned on our goals: get This Man naked and into high gear as the sex animal that he most certainly is, and I'll watch and take notes.

I told This Woman that she was going to have to be assertive if sex was going to happen at all. I suggested that she ask him to take a sauna with her, and she'd go in and get things warmed up with him, and then I could come in and watch and maybe … maybe join in. She agreed, and as he came out of the shower stall, in her extreme position of feminine power, she said to him in the most lilting way, "Is the sauna on? Why don't you turn it on and get it ready for us?"

He was about to get dressed figuring it was all over for the evening, but then I could see his face light up in the dark as he dropped his clothes in a pile and set off to the sauna with a hopeful spring in his step. There's nothing like a man who has been given the next green light toward the big pink light he desires more than anything.

They went in. I stayed in the pool and about 20 minutes later I joined them in the sauna. They were already at second base—he was on the upper bench and she was beneath him getting a neck, shoulder and breast massage. Good work, I thought. You two are moving right along as planned. I lay down next to them with my head against her thigh and held his hairy leg. I could see he was already erect and pointing up the back of her neck. She was moaning and breathing heavily.

Strangely I found *her* kinda sexy—not so much the architecture—but the erotic power and energy that she put out was intense and enveloping. I got kind of lost in petting her sweaty body almost as much as I did in rubbing his legs and reaching around to cup his butt. I started massaging her just to turn *him* on—another guy helping himself to what should naturally be his, figuring this will inspire a bit of healthy competition. In actuality, I kind of enjoyed hearing her respond with little moans of pleasure. Surely I was not going to turn him on, but maybe I would her. And that was appealing in its own way.

Next, she turned around and went down on him. I got the full view of him in his erotic glory—hard and ready with his youthful muscles dimly glistening in the darkened sauna. I slowly inched my hands further up his thighs and reached for his nuts. I enclosed the hairy orbs in my fingers and he twitched just a little—could this be his first time being touched by a man? He didn't bolt and she didn't stop blowing him and the heat kept rising. This Woman and I were a team of pleasure for This Man and he had surrendered to it.

Alas, I knew that at some point I had worked myself out of a job. Playing impresario for these two was a necessary role to get to this point, and I had my fun and got my story. A graceful retreat on my part was now necessary if I was going to leave with some dignity. They took a break and we each hugged and kissed goodbye.

This Man stayed for a moment after she left and in a very sensitive but firm way he said, "Sorry man, but you know I'm into *her*."

"I know. Have a great time," I said as he left, his bare butt and hard-on gleaming in the light. I knew the score—my entire childhood prepared me for this evening.

I stayed in the sauna reading through my mental notes, rearranging my thoughts like one would pictures in a collage. Hmmm, how should I look at this? What really *is* the story here? Was this a repeat of my adolescent fascination with all the unavailable boys? Or was this a very intimate encounter with a man and a woman and I need not run it through with my own drama about neglect? I was having a bit of a hard time with it—but in the end, I'm sorry to report, I chose the former.

This Man came back for something he had left and he came over to me and shook my hand as real men are supposed to do. I think hugging a naked guy was just too much for him. As I was getting dressed, he said, "Let's continue this connection."

"Hey, I've held your nuts now, so the hard part is over. And there's a certain truth in that. I'll be around," I told him. He smiled and walked off toward the parking lot with the confident stride of a lion who got his meal.

As I went to the parking lot, I saw them by her car, making out beneath a flowering plumeria tree—a scene about as lovely as Hawaii can provide. I slipped into my car and then passed them walking down the driveway holding hands. I felt a strong twinge of envy for that affection, that infatuation. Certainly I've been in their position many times in my life and there's no need to be greedy. Just admire it, I thought. So I rolled down the window and as I passed them, I said, "You two are *so* beautiful."

This Woman said, "So are *you,* David."

As I was rolling up the window I said a little bit to them, but mostly to myself, "I know." I lied to them a little bit, but mostly I lied to myself.

Back at my house I lay in bed naked trying to feel something and re-arranging those thoughts again. A close encounter with such beautiful people in that state of arousal is powerfully intoxicating. I felt somehow desirous and yet absent of any ability to do anything about it with myself, or anyone.

Emptiness became the collage of images collected that evening. It was a night of men paying no attention to me, and the one man who did, by nature had to shut me out. I felt no blame for him—actually I kind of felt bad for him. He clearly enjoyed the emotional intimacy of a man; he just didn't want it to go further. And I can't fault him for that. We are both following our instincts to a fork—he got the girl and I got the story. I imagined him inside her as I lay there listening to Monkey Pod having a dream in the living room and watching my fan beat slowly in front of the puffy clouds I had painstakingly painted on my bedroom ceiling.

Lying in the darkness surrounded by the four walls bearing my hard work, I felt comforted but it didn't feel like home. Alone with my things to soothe me, I have come to realize that the soft sheets of my bed, the gentle whirring of the fan—all that I have built and sweat and paid for so dearly—are comforts that will not leave me with a cursory handshake. My four walls won't walk away while I'm talking to them. But all of this won't amount to a cuddle, a kiss, or a tender fuck. And those four walls could be anywhere.

And so at last I have my sign.

Love, Seaweed

23

November 28, 2006

ALOHA `OE VEY

A man travels the world over in search of what he needs
and returns home to find it.
—George Moore

My adventure to the jungles and lava fields of Hawaii began with a
few scratches on the back of an envelope at my friend Don's jungalow in Kehena Beach in February 2005. I scrawled out the prelimi-
nary design of a home I would build on a 7,500 square foot piece of
jagged a'a in the middle of a field of wild orchids with a view of the
Pacific Ocean. I then drew it up in a graphics program on the computer.

A year and a half-later, under the very roof of the house I had
sketched, I find myself taping boxes and zipping up my suitcase in
the living room, shipping my life back to myself on the mainland.
My boxes were bound for home—a surprise twist—an unexpected
spin of the compass, sending me back where I began, to the kitty litter landscapes of the desert. I had not expected to call Tucson home,
ever again.

I could not ignore the call to adventure, and now I must heed the call home. Certainly no one has ever accused me of being a restful person. The restlessness that led me one day to get in the car and drive to Arizona from San Francisco also led me to Hawaii, fleeing the strip-mall sprawl of the desert city. And once again it put me on a plane for the mainland US with my pots and pans following by ship.

Searching for the ever-elusive concept of home has been an exhausting, fascinating, and in the end, futile journey across oceans and deserts. The unsatisfying results of my quest have left me bereft, geographically confused, thinking that I will never find my home. But since my return to Tucson, I have found myself deeply grounded by the daily routine, the solidness and predictability of my life here. All the things I once fled now were comforting to me after a year of the challenges of building a house thousands of miles away in Hawaii.

A couple weeks ago, in the warm Arizona morning sun, I stepped out into the front courtyard to saddle up on my bicycle and head to the farmer's market and behold—that sought after moment arrived—a moment when I knew I was in the right place at the right time and that for once in my tireless travails, I had a clear and palpable sense of home.

You know those posters you see of "The Doors of (whatever city)"—those idyllic pictures of a locale's thresholds where you think to yourself, "Oh that's just too precious and if only I were there sitting on that stoop, then I'd be happy and I'd know I was home?" Well, that moment came to me, only this time, *gasp,* it was on my very own doorstep. I daresay that I wouldn't have had that epiphany had I not gone to such extremes seeking exactly what I now know I have here in Tucson.

As the billowy orange clouds of yet another stunning desert sunset cross over the house, I look out my home office window and greet the dusk with a phrase that I keep hearing echo in my head, "They'll take me out of here in a coffin." One should never believe lines like that with me for *too* long, but for the moment it rings true (even as I search the web for cheap accommodations in Thailand—my next conquest).

But how much can I go on and on about how much I love my home in Tucson before I become an utter bore? I think I crossed that bridge about five minutes ago. Wasn't Hawaii so much more colorful and interesting with its parade of characters living on the edge of insanity? Thomas Moore wrote, "The ordinary acts we practice every day at home are of more importance to the soul than their simplicity might suggest." Amen.

I can't tell you how satisfying it is (after having sets of keys to various friends' houses and cars in California and Hawaii) to have just my own keys, all identified and hanging on a rack in the utility closet in the order of their daily use. It doesn't make for very good reading to hear about how delighted I am that I bike to the farmer's market on Sunday, and the woman behind the bread table scratches her initials on my frequent buyer card and that in just eight more loaves, I get a free one. How fabulous is it to know that I finally unpacked my toiletries and put them in a drawer and that I stopped living out of my suitcase and stored it below the staircase, and to know that each afternoon I watch Charlie Rose while I have lunch, read, and then fall asleep for my afternoon nap?

The simplest details of my life give me enormous comfort after having spent a year standing on roof joists nailing purlins in the rain, battling crazy people about their vicious dogs, watching people let flies eat out their staph infections, venturing into the slimy jungles to silence coqui frogs in their endless imperative to destroy the tranquility of Hawaii. It was an amazing adventure, but everything has its cycles and now I'm in a deep state of domestic contraction.

I returned to Hawaii from the mainland in August to see if there was much of a life for me and to deal with my beloved dog, Monkey Pod. At that time I still had not decided for sure that I couldn't live in Hawaii, but my last two months in Puna were rather telling. I spent far too many quiet nights by myself sitting in the hammock with Monkey, watching the cruise ship light up the sky on its passage to see Kilauea bleeding into the ocean only a few miles down the coast. I imagine the ship listing to one side as all the obese people line the decks to peer out at an erupting volcano before the midnight buffet. Monkey Pod, however, watches me wondering if he's going to get his version of the midnight buffet.

Ugh! This is impossible—this romantic notion of lying in the hammock by oneself. Sorry Monkey Pod, you don't count. Watching cruise ships on a tropical island … it's lovely, really. But how many nights can I do this before I resort to screaming into the jungle like my neighbors? How many nights alone before I turn into my neighbor with the restraining orders, tormenting people who leave him always locked outside the community. I think that lone coqui frog next door and I have more in common than I thought: I spared his life when I finally understood that in his own limited musical vocabulary, he was calling for a mate to come be with him in the jungle.

On this night, however, the phone rang. It was the velvety-smooth voice of Kimberly at the other end, "David Darling, someone gave me a joint as payment for a yoga class I taught at Kalani. Do you want to come over and smoke it with me?" Sitting in someone's jungalow getting stoned is not really my idea of a stimulating evening. It has always seemed more like medicating away the deadly loneliness of living so isolated a life. But never one to turn down an invitation from Kimberly, I accepted.

Kimberly, as scholar, writer and performer, is one of the most unlikely inhabitants of the damp jungles of Puna. I suppose that really is what Puna is all about—the weird juxtapositions that leave you either smiling or shocked or both. Driving around in my 2005 Scion I realized that I was not doing my part to keep Puna weird. So I drove with my seatbelt unfastened a couple of times—that was about all I could muster. Yeah, Gilmore, unbuckle that belt and live dangerously. Just let yourself go, hon. I think driving a new car was considered weird for Puna.

Tonight, though, I wanted to embrace the favorite pastime of the locals—pakalolo. I snapped on my headlamp, slipped the leash around Monkey Pod's head and set out for Kimberly's house. Kimberly lives in a cute cottage right at the edge of a dense jungle—as if her house were caught in the mouth of a green giant trying to gobble it up. With serious weed whacking, she seems to keep the house wrested from the jaws of the wild beast.

Monkey Pod sat on Kimberly's porch while I went inside to light up. I wondered if this could be the first time I smoked pakalolo in Hawaii. After a few minutes of sucking in the stinky smoke, Kimberly and I began laughing and talking endlessly with brains disengaged from mouths—speaking long sentences at the end of which, I couldn't remember what the beginning was.

Suddenly, revelation of revelations, the isolation and the discord with the Puna-vibe vanished! The jaws of the jungle opened wide and exhaled its laughing gas on us. Everything began to make sense: the bird lady, the guy who goes around and around on the scooter, the guy playing the theme song to *The Flintstones* over and over again on the saxophone, Yellin' Helen, and the entire cast of weirdoes that populate lower Puna.

It was all perfectly right, albeit state-specific. If you don't have a café to go to, if you can't stop by the bistro on the way home from work and have a little pasta with your friends, catch an art film, then the next best thing is to lie back on your moldy sofa with a big old fatty dangling from your lips while a cloud of blue smoke circles around your slack-jawed head.

We went out for a walk with Monkey Pod leading the way in the moonlight. He would disappear in various empty lots for a few minutes but always returned to take the lead. We sauntered down the Seaview grid in awe of the bright moonlight on the roofs of houses, which, in our altered state, made them appear snow-covered.

I began to feel the remorse of someone who comes to the end of his life only to realize he simply had not lived. Perhaps when you arrive at the Hilo airport, they should slap a sticky homegrown joint in your mouth instead of a flower lei over your head. I think if that had been done, I might still be there lying on the floor with Monkey Pod listening to my neighbor playing *The Flintstones* theme song and thinking it was damn good.

But they didn't. And I didn't. I passed out in some sort of mollified state that honestly, I can't remember—another useful side effect of pakalolo. Hey, if you don't remember that you passed out stoned last night, then you're guiltlessly allowed to do it again tonight. It was after that night with Kimberly and the joint that I decided that I just couldn't toe it in Puna any longer. My island life was coming to an end.

I found myself dreaming of urban environments—opera houses, teeming wharves, esplanades, crowds of people I didn't know, facilities for the mentally ill, lace-up shoes. The walls of Puna began closing in, there's not a shoe store for 35 miles, and I had to get out. I could not face another night at the lousy Mexican restaurant in Pahoa with the rough crowds tripping on their slippahs walking the decrepit streets of Pahoa.

Aloha, Oy Vey.

Moving toward the end of my Hawaiian chapter, I threw myself a going away picnic on the lawn one Sunday afternoon by the ocean in front of the Seaview neighborhood. We assembled on blankets and were uncorking wine and eating our potluck lunch watching rainstorms and rainbows form and dissipate over the ocean when a pickup truck driven by Kurt, the neighbor with multiple restraining orders on him, pulled aggressively in front of us, practically parking on the blankets. We all leaned back, clutching our crackers and goat cheese, bracing ourselves for what was to come.

Kurt has a history of violent aggressions against his ex-boyfriend who happened to be joining us. When they split up, Kurt's brain snapped and he went on rampages in the neighborhood, targeting gay men and friends of his ex for lectures on the evils of promiscuity. We sat silently on the blanket waiting for our mass execution, Columbine-style. I stood up getting ready to bolt.

Kurt, a deceivingly handsome guy with salt and pepper hair, big green eyes and a solid, muscular body, jumped out of the truck and came right over to me with a crooked smile working up the side of his face. Hmmm. I wondered if he was on some new meds and was going to be uncharacteristically docile. He extended his hand to me. Caught off guard I extended mine back to him slowly, firming up my stance on the ground in case he was going to try to yank me off my feet. I have never given him any reason to dislike me other than that I have befriended his ex, if that's considered just cause for hostility.

"I hear you're leaving—glad to hear it. Good riddance. And take these *bitches* with you," he said as he gestured to the rest of the party. He gave us all the evil eye then turned on his heels and walked back to the truck. He tore up a little patch of grass as he sped away.

We all silently looked to his ex for an interpretation, who was rolling his eyes and shaking his head in disbelief at Kurt's latest outburst of Sturm und Drang. He nervously laughed at this near-violent encounter, but I couldn't. I was angry. This moron had ruined my going away picnic and there was not a thing we could do about it. Seems anything I do in Puna, my peaceful enjoyment is almost always encroached upon by some lunatic who wants to throw a rock, sing out of key, commandeer a conversation, scream in the jungle, yell at a community meeting, or make a scene in public.

"Well, if I had any doubts about leaving …" I smirked to my friends who seemed wide-eyed and waiting to hear what I had to say about this.

"I give up on him. I've tried to help him, but that's it. He's just a lost cause," Bill said, throwing up his arms in frustration.

"Aw, come on. Just ignore him," his ex told us.

"How do I know he's not going to come to *my* house and kick my door down like he did *yours?* And what have I ever done to him to deserve that?" I asked, still quivering from the encounter.

"Well, consider yourself lucky. He ran Devin off the road thinking he was one of the porn stars who were here shooting a film at the beach," Stevie added. We all groaned.

"Well, how about a drink?" Rainer said uncorking some wine.

Even after a couple glasses of wine, I was still unable to find some levity at the picnic and had to keep an eye out for Kurt's truck in between watching the rainbows. What if he went to get a gun and was going to return to mow us all down?

One of the passing rain showers was destined for our picnic blanket. The blue of the roiling sea turned gray as it worked its way toward us dragging a white silky net of rain over the cliffs and up the grassy lawn toward us with a rainbow clinging to its right edge. Stevie opened a large black umbrella. Monkey Pod stood by sniffing the grass. Max leaned back on his elbow. The figures all came into place, and it struck me that we had accidentally recreated Georges Seurat's famous *Sunday on the Island of La Grande Jatte* painting. Monkey Pod took off after a bird, but I captured the rest of it in a picture just before the rain drenched us.

Monkey Pod and I spent the next day alone together—as usual—with the wind whispering among the ferns and orchid fields. I quietly contemplated what to do with him. I let him in from the lanai. He quickly glanced up at me for direction. I snapped his cue to jump up on the day bed and he began earnestly thumping his tail inviting me to cuddle with him on the bed. I laid down next to him. He put his head gently on my chest and I looked into his eyes and said to him, "No matter where you go, you know that I love you, right?" He blinked a few times and closed his eyes and fell asleep. His breath was heavy and his paws twitched as he was having doggy dreams. I watched the ceiling fan slowly turning for a long time.

After several weeks of putting out flyers and sending the word out on the coconut wireless that Monkey Pod needs a home, finally a suitable foster parent responded and I agreed to give him away.

When I found Monkey Pod on the street, a year earlier, he had been neglected to the point that his blood was teeming with microfilaria—the baby heartworms. His heart, by deduction, was infested with spaghetti-sized worms. I opted out of toxic arsenic treatments and instead put him on preventive pills and exercised him hard. I made him run after the car and bicycle and had him pull me around the tide pools by his tail—to strengthen his heart.

Before I left the island, I made an appointment at the veterinarian's office to check him for heartworms. His new owner Henry, an older gay man with a soft spot for black Labs, accompanied me to the vet. If all checked out OK, Henry would take Monkey Pod. I was very nervous in anticipation of the results. I could not let the Humane Society destroy him—as they do with any dog with heartworms, and I was not sure Henry would take him if he tested positive. I could not imagine or even afford to take Monkey back to Arizona—he would be stuck indoors in a housing complex—not much of a life for a dog that grew up running free in the jungle chasing mongooses.

For a couple months after taking the prevention pills and the exercise, Monkey coughed and sputtered. He must have been kicking the worms out because when I went to peer into the microscope at the vet's office this time, the orange slide of his blood was clear. No worms! Triumphantly, I walked out to greet Henry in the lobby with a rapturous smile, knowing that the handoff of a healthy dog was about to occur. If I had done nothing else positive on this yearlong crucible in Hawaii, I had cured Monkey of his fatal ailment.

The three of us stood in the parking lot beaming. I took a few steps back from Henry and unhitched Monkey Pod's leash from his collar. Henry started toward his truck to leave. Monkey gave us each a look and paused. Then he excitedly headed toward Henry's truck. I waved goodbye to them for the last time as they pulled out of the rainy parking lot. After I returned to Tucson, Henry called me a couple times to tell me how grateful he was to have such an extraordinary dog. Monkey sniffed the receiver when I called his name. Henry reported that they were going to class together to learn a few things about obedience. Something I suppose even a dog could get into.

It was strange to return back to the house that had never been without Monkey Pod, to open the door and not have a bundle of black fur throw itself on me with uninhibited glee. Monkey had sat patiently for months as the house was under way, tied to the construction tent with the builders' dogs. I kind of missed seeing the eerie blue glow of his eyes over the lanai railing caught in my headlights as I approached the house after dark. The house now seemed deadly silent.

I felt a slight twinge of disloyalty for having given him away. It seemed I was tearing down my traveling circus tent fast. I eased my guilt remembering that Monkey Pod and I have one thing in common: wanderlust. His new home with Henry would afford him the luxury of space—to chase chickens and cats up trees at will. There would be no more sitting on the lanai waiting for me to come home.

My final night in Hawaii was, of course, a rainy one. I invited a handful of friends to join me at Kalani for aloha dinner. It was a mixture of straight and gay friends I had met and become close to, even if at the last minute as was the case with Kevin, Tuko, and Craig. John and Harlan, the building angels, were not there. Sadly, a few months ago, they sold their houses and moved to Texas. It was terribly painful to hug them goodbye for the last time with my debt of gratitude unpaid. They wanted to live with just a little more civilization, closer to doctors.

Tonight, at the final hour, I was delighted to feel a sense of belonging. Looking around the table at this group of smart, open-hearted, creative friends, I had just a moment of pause wondering if I was doing the right thing. Seeing the Kalani cliques giggling amongst themselves confirmed that it was the right decision. At 42, I was a pesky old man from the neighborhood as seen through the blinkered eyes of the prancing twinkies who comprise the bulk of the workforce of Kalani.

After dinner we went to the hot tub and pool and swam naked under a dark tropical sky—with stars appearing in between passing rain showers. Afterward, Craig and Stevie accompanied me to the parking lot. I stopped on the fork of the path to our cars. I hugged them each goodbye and said walking away, "I love you guys." This was a bit bold for me—I'm not used to telling people I love them so casually, but it does seem to be the Hawaiian way, and I might as well get with the program on the last night.

"We love you too, David," I heard from Stevie. It gave me a warm feeling—even if *this* definition of love might not stand the test of time. But who knows?

You know, leaving really is very satisfying—you get taken out to dinner and people tell you all the things that, had they told you earlier, you might not be leaving. But you can't tinker with this—you have to die to get your eulogy—you have to leave to get the farewell parties.

Queen Lili'uokalani wrote this famous song of farewell. I downloaded it from iTunes and played it for myself before I left for the airport:

> *Aloha `oe, aloha `oe*
> *E ke onaona noho i ka lipo.*
> *a ho`i a`e au*
> *A hui hou aku.*
>
> *Farewell to thee, farewell to thee*
> *O fragrance in the blue depths.*
> *One fond embrace and I leave*
> *To meet again.*

A Brief Aside on the Concept of Home

What is *home,* really? What makes a house or a place feel like a home to you? Perhaps you can begin to deconstruct the myth of it by answering this seemingly simple question in sober, unsentimental terms. Your answer might be something like: home is a place where someone will be making me dinner when I return from work; or home is a place that has a piano; or home is a place where I can take a walk and see people in a public square.

Once you begin to dissect the lofty concept of home into simpler terms, then you can address it in more practical ways: why not invite someone to cook you dinner? Better yet, go cook someone else dinner when they return from work; or go piano shopping today; or get yourself a bicycle and head to the park or your local downtown. The concept of home left unexamined in nebulous, romantic terms is useful material for writing a bleeding-heart book or the subject of a song, but you'll end up chasing rainbows like I have done and ultimately discovering that you're running out of road. I ran out of road in Hawaii, but not before making a colossal mess.

I have gotten a lot of artistic mileage out of my wistful wanderings, and join ranks with some of my favorite writers and musicians who work that same nerve. Home is a universal theme for us humans, isn't it? (Oh dear, I hope you don't feel cheated for having bought this book and reached the end only to find that there may actually be a redeeming message.)

It's the final piece of wisdom in L. Frank Baum's *The Wonderful Wizard of Oz.* Dorothy goes off in a dream to her version of my Hawaii complete with wicked witches and flying monkeys. I found wicked neighbors and flying roaches, but it's all the same. And she finally awakened after clicking her ruby flip-flops, er, slippahs to find that *home,* dear ones, was not so far away at all.

Looking back at my life in Seaview, I think I was once again naïvely thinking that home was always somewhere else. John Lennon said something like, "Life is what happens when you're busy making other plans." I think Tucson was happening while I was planning Hawaii. I feel sorry for my poor friends who witness me endlessly searching for something better. I have at last come to realize that my sense of home is not tied to a structure and not tied to any one place. And what a relief that is.

Somehow, I thought that life on an exotic, tropical island might relieve me of the invisibility of middle age … that life there on the edge of civilization would be a better plan for the second half of my life—an escape strategy for the pain of being ignored. How could it be? How could any place or people possibly live up to my expectations?

Instead I'm in the desert watching movies in my beloved back house, playing Rufus Wainwright songs on the piano, which I have to say, is far better than listening to my neighbor playing *The Flintstones* theme song on his saxophone.

Six weeks after returning to Arizona, my boxes arrived mostly undamaged, though my cell phone was missing. I unpacked my mildewed clothes and shoes with a bit of nostalgia. I brushed the green fungi off my red suede shoes and hoped that my clothes didn't spill any roach eggs on the way to the washer. Any spores that returned with me will soon be dead in the dry desert air. I managed to steam the dents out of my straw hat. Holding the hat over a boiling kettle of water, the steam released a distinct smell of the jungle, opening up a chest full of memories of my year in Hawaii.

Love and aloha,

Dorothy

EPILOGUE

More than a year has passed since the final inspection of the house and I think I am at long last over my post construction stress disorder, not that I would ever build a house again. It wasn't a transition marked by some event or epiphany. One hardly notices when something stops hurting. My resentments of the contractors leaving me to finish the house, the onus of the mistakes I made, the environmental damage, and then there's the dashed romantic dreams of a home in paradise … the nightmares of it all have at last loosened their grip on me.

Finally, after a year of recovery, I am willing to concede that the house I built is a beautiful house. Friends have sent me pictures of it, ironically with rainbows arching over its cute little Balinese roof. Building it was admittedly over-ambitious for a single person and a 135-pound weakling at that. It is without any doubt, the most difficult project I have ever taken on. And it is done. Fait accompli.

I am, however, still recovering from the financial drain of the construction. I have stripped my life down to the basics giving up my cell phone, health insurance, gym membership, and my Tucson car. Then, with the last bit of savings I had after the sale of the Hawaii car, I installed a photovoltaic solar system on the house in Tucson, as a conciliatory gesture to the environment for my transgressions in Hawaii.

My enthusiasm for Tucson and the mainland has somewhat tapered off over the year of being back. Much of this is due to a growing resentment of America and its aggressive imperialism, and not specifically about Tucson. I have felt another wave or restlessness moving through me, and this time it reaches beyond America's shores to Asia—to a place where at my age, I'm really just starting to become attractive to beautiful young men.

In the winter of 2007, I rewarded myself for finishing the house construction by using up the frequent flyer miles I accumulated for charging building materials to my credit card and took off for Thailand. I didn't anticipate liking the Thai people as much as I did. I came back from my trip enamored and eager to return.

Touring around the Thai islands near Krabi, I thought about Hawaii by comparison. Thailand has the distinction of never having been colonized, and so its language and culture are still intact. Unlike the Hawaiians, whose language and culture have all but disappeared with the American occupation, the Thai people have no palpable resentment of tourists. They welcome foreigners with smiles and bows.

I felt my interest in Hawaii drifting even further away. I even started fantasizing about being an ex-pat American living in Thailand, having a Thai boyfriend. Oh god, not a repeat of that whole thing again. This time, I laughed and caught myself before I started thinking about selling the Tucson house and packing boxes. I hope that if I learned anything from my experience in Hawaii, I learned that nurturing a sense of home wherever I am is a better survival skill than running away.

It's fascinating to see the look of incredulity on people's faces when you tell them you much prefer Tucson to Hawaii. But those who have lived there and returned to the mainland know exactly what I'm talking about. Those who have only visited Hawaii call it "island fever." I'm not sure that's what my malaise was. I guess I always thought island fever would be a burning feeling that you have to get off this tiny island because the walls are closing in, that you long for the open road or a vast tract of land. I didn't feel that. I don't long for road trips. I live fairly close-in with my village life in

Tucson. I simply was tired of the insularity of always seeing the same people and yet not feeling a deep sense of belonging. I grew tired of eating at the same restaurants, the lack of worldly perspective, and doing the same things over and over. If that's island fever, then I guess I had it. *Bad.*

Nonetheless those with thicker skin, a stronger constitution, or a better-stocked medicine cabinet manage to happily call Hawaii home. It's as if the spirit of the island must first break you down and then if you've kept your wits about you, you can stay. Hawaii rose up from the ocean floor as volcanic lava cooled, finally pushing the islands to the surface. For millions of years there was nothing but rock. Over the millennia, birds blown off course in storms landed on the islands bringing seeds from foreign lands. Seedpods floating from other islands washed up on shore and took root. But not everything that lands on Hawaii's shores survives.

ABOUT THE AUTHOR

David Gilmore was the host and executive producer of *Outright Radio,* a story-based public radio show he started with Tom Truss, Scott Jones, and Joan Schuman at KUSP, in Santa Cruz in 1998. The show was featured on Public Radio International (PRI) from 2000 to 2005, won the Edward R. Murrow Award, the Golden and Silver Reels from the National Federation of Community Broadcasters, and was funded by the Corporation for Public Broadcasting. In addition to being a National Endowment for the Arts grantee for the radio show, Gilmore also made a short film about gay male body image obsessions called *Ideal Man,* which was shown in select gay and lesbian film festivals around the nation in 2005. Archives of these projects are available at www.outrightradio.org and www.outrightvideo.org, respectively.

Currently, he writes and photographs for his blog at www.nineteenthparallel.com, and has contributed articles and essays to *Advocate.com* and *The Gay & Lesbian Review.* His short films can be seen on YouTube by searching for DavidGilmore, and he can be reached at: david@outrightradio.org.

978-0-595-45473-0
0-595-45473-9

CPSIA information can be obtained
at www.ICGtesting.com
Printed in the USA
LVHW041130140623
749721LV00003B/27